HOW TO MEET YOUR PERFECT MATCH

*Includes Over 50 Tried and Tested Strategies You Need
To Attract a Relationship That Works*

CANDY JANNETTA

Published by Essencial Publishing

Second edition, 2014

Candy Jannetta, Copyright © 2009

Candy Jannetta has asserted her moral right under the Copyright, Designs and Patents Act 1988 to be identified as author of this work.

A CIP catalogue record for this book is available from the British Library

ISBN 978-0-9570235-0-5

The author and the publisher have made every effort to seek permission from all those quoted to reproduce their words. If you believe that any quotation violates a copyright you hold or represent, we will immediately remove it upon notification pending good faith resolution of any dispute, and seek to rectify any errors in any subsequent editions.

All rights reserved. No part of this book may be reproduced, stored in a retrieval system, or transmitted by any means, electronic, mechanical, photocopying, recorded or otherwise without written permission from the publisher.

Book Cover Design by Jem Butcher
Photography by Katy McDonnell
Typeset by Electric Reads (www.electricreads.com)

info@howtomeetyourperfectmatch.com
www.howtomeetyourperfectmatch.com

TABLE OF CONTENTS

Introduction 7
   About this book 9
   How to use this book 11

Chapter 1 12
How to overcome destructive relationship patterns
   Step 1: Gain awareness of your relationship patterns 14
   Step 2: Understand why you are repeating these patterns 30
   Step 3: Identify the warning signals of your destructive patterns 34
   Step 4: Create an image of a healthy relationship for yourself 38
   Step 5: Build your self-esteem 40
   Step 6: Say no! 43

Chapter 2 44
Letting go of past relationships to make way for future ones
   Ten signs you are holding on to a past relationship 44
   Three tough truths 45
   How to let go of past relationships 45

Chapter 3 55
Your perfect match – what's holding you back
Common limiting beliefs about relationships 55
What is a belief? 58
How you can overcome your limiting beliefs 59

Chapter 4 67
How to get the relationship you want
Why you need to know what you want in a relationship 68
The four problems with making a list 68
How to identify what you want 70
Core values – their importance and how they impact on your relationships 77
Why having a shared vision is so important 83
How to ensure you don't attract another Mr or Mrs Wrong 84
When you should discover if your date is a potential perfect match 85
How you can work out if your date is a potential perfect match 87
How to identify if you share any core values 90
How to identify if you share a similar vision 91

Chapter 5 92
Building dating confidence
Is lack of confidence affecting your chances of meeting your perfect match? 93

How to feel confident about who you are ...96
How to feel confident about your appearance..100
How to feel confident about your appeal to the opposite sex..104
Recommended reading...............................122

Chapter 6 123
Dating success
How to attract and approach the opposite sex..124
How to communicate confidence through body language...125
What to do when you feel confident and have the other person's attention.................129
How to handle and deal out rejection 130
How to make the most of first dates...........133
What to say on a first date...........................133
What to wear on a first date........................135
Where to go on a first date 135
What do you do at the end of a date?.........136
Do you kiss on a first date? 137
How to behave in the initial dating stages.138
Surviving the infatuation stage...................140

Chapter 7 143
Where and how to meet your perfect match
How to create a dating strategy 145
Where to meet the opposite sex 145
Where not to meet the opposite sex............152
How to get the most out of online dating..153
Online dating myths 154

Overcoming your barriers to online dating 155
The advantages of online dating 156
The dos and don'ts of online dating 157
Writing your online profile 159
Your online photo 166
Creating the right username 168
Choosing the right dating site 169
Online love stories 172
How to get the most out of speed dating ... 175
How speed dating works 175
The dos and don'ts of speed dating 176
How to get the most out of introduction agencies 178
Dos and don'ts of using an introduction agency 180

Chapter 8 182
Maximizing your chances of meeting your perfect match

Eight ways to stay motivated while searching for your perfect match 182
The fourteen mistakes to avoid in the early stages of a relationship 187
How to tell if he/she is into you 188
Fourteen ways to maintain a healthy relationship 190
Why you should never give up on your dream of meeting your perfect match 195

Disclaimer 198

Acknowledgements 200

INTRODUCTION

Dear Reader,

Thank you for buying this book and well done for taking an important step towards meeting your perfect match.

I have seen and met increasing numbers of men and women who, like you, are looking for more than a companion or partner; they are looking for their perfect match. It took me more than 15 years to meet my perfect match and I had a hard time along the way. Now every single day I can't believe my luck to be waking up next to my beautiful, loving and perfect husband. My mission in life is to help as many people as possible to experience the happiness I have found and meet their special someone.

I spent 13 and a half out of my 21 adult years as a single woman and have been in destructive as well as good relationships. It was not until I changed fundamental things within myself that I met my current husband. Here is a brief summary of the journey which led me to where I am now.

In my early 20's I was happily footloose and fancy-free and was more interested in travelling than a serious relationship. Then in my mid-twenties I decided that I wanted less casual relationships but fell for someone who was already in a relationship and who I let treat me disrespectfully. I became addicted to the thrill of being with someone who wasn't totally available and ended up getting very hurt. This relationship left me angry and with strong feelings of not being worthy. Self-development tools and good friends helped me to get through this period.

Two years later, I started to form healthier relationships but most of them were short-lived and I became increasingly disillusioned with relationships. Spending long hours at my job became an excuse not to do anything about my personal life. This left me feeling lonely and stressed. A trip to New Zealand gave me the inspiration to make some changes in my life. You may know the expression: "be careful what you wish for". I came back from my trip with a focus on fun and my wish came true. I started meeting men much younger than me who were interested in having fun. This made me realize that I wanted more than just fun.

On February 14th, 2003, I went to a party and noticed a man at the bar who I thought was the most beautiful man I had seen in a long time. To my surprise, he came over to me and said, "Did you feel the energy between us?" The connection between us grew from there and we spent three happy months together. We both knew and admitted to each other that we were soul mates. This man had sickle cell anemia which is a life-threatening condition.

When I met him he was well but had previously spent long periods in hospital. One night I was with him while he was getting over a sickle cell crisis and I woke up to find him dead. I'm telling you this since it really was a turning point in my life and tested my faith and determination. People said to me: "you'll never meet anyone like that again" and "you're so unlucky in love". These negative comments made me more determined to meet another soul mate and someone who would play a different part in my life.

After a period of intense grieving, I decided to focus on meeting my perfect match. I spent time observing fulfilled relationships, was coached to overcome deeply entrenched barriers and tried every kind of dating option out there – speed dating, blind dates, internet dating and the traditional club and bar hopping. At the age of 35 and after several stabs at internet dating, I met my now husband online. We were so sure that we were right for each other that we got married within eight months of knowing each other. Neither of us has looked back since.

About this book

This book is the culmination of my personal experience and everything I have learned from running more than 50 Meet Your Perfect Match workshops and coaching hundreds of single clients whom I have had the pleasure of working with.

Imagine what your life would be like if you were waking up every morning and coming home every night to your special someone. Imagine your life with no more lonely Saturday nights, no more holidays on your own, no more weddings and parties on your own. Imagine how much more you could give and achieve with the support of a loving partner.

As you read this book, you will gain the motivation, inspiration and tools to help you find the love you deserve.

> ### Gill's story
>
> "Dear Candy,
>
> I attended your workshop and found it a most uplifting and enjoyable day. It gave me the courage not to settle for second best. For the past 10 years, since my last long-term relationship, I had had a few relationships. Your workshop made me realize that they were all destined to fail for various reasons and wish that I had previously had the insight to move on sooner.
>
> I had been on dating websites on and off for several years and then one day Bill's picture popped up. He had such nice eyes and his profile was witty and genuine. We began emailing daily and with every message I became increasingly excited and convinced that I had found someone very special. We met for lunch two weeks later and then a couple of days later drove to France for New Year. We both felt as if we had always been friends, we just hadn't met yet. I know that I have found my soul mate and that we will be together indefinitely.
>
> After a year and a half we are still completely besotted with each other and as happy as ever. Bill is actually even more wonderful than I first realized!
>
> I always thought that this kind of thing happened to other people and not me, but it did, at 51 years old. Thanks, Gill."

Most of my clients come to me desperate to know the secrets of how and where to meet potential partners. They want to launch themselves straight into the dating stage without doing any prior thought or preparation. What would happen if you desperately wanted to change jobs and you went straight to any kind of interview you could get without working out what kind of job you want, salary or location, without carefully writing a CV to sell yourself, without researching companies and without preparing questions for interview? You would fail miserably and either be rejected at the interview or end up with a job which you hated. Likewise, if you do no preparation to meet your perfect match you could end up being rejected or in a relationship you hate.

How to use this book

The first six chapters of this book provide you with the necessary steps to prepare and lead you to your perfect match. The seventh chapter covers where and how to meet potentials. The eighth chapter shows you how to maximize your chances of meeting your perfect match, maintain the relationship you deserve and never to give up!

This book is packed with tried and tested tools, if you really want to meet your perfect match, read them, read them again and apply them. If you feel you need extra assistance and support, don't hesitate to contact me to find out how my workshops and coaching could help you. I have also included lots of real-life examples and success stories to prove that finding your perfect match is possible.

I have included book recommendations so that you can get more in-depth knowledge and understanding of certain relationship areas.

I wish you the best of luck in the search for your perfect match. It makes my day when readers share their success stories after following this book so do get in touch. I also welcome any feedback you may have about this book.

Good luck!
Candy

Chapter I

How to overcome destructive relationship patterns

"Continuing to do the same things, hoping for a different outcome."

— Einstein's definition of madness

If you carry on doing the same things and adopting the same attitudes towards relationships, you will achieve the same outcomes which will continue to make you unhappy.

This chapter will help you identify the mistakes you have been repeating and, most importantly, give you the tools to overcome these mistakes.

Psychologists estimate that between **birth and 5 years of age**, you receive **50% of your emotional programming.**

Psychologists estimate that between **5 and 8 years of age**, you receive **30% of your emotional programming.**

From the age of 0 to 5 years old, your parents are the centre of your world so the majority of programming comes from them, with some from siblings, other close relatives and friends.

From the age of 5 to 8 years old, you are still highly influenced by your parents, with some additional influence from peers, siblings, close relatives and friends.

Psychologists estimate that between the **ages of 8 and 18** you receive **15%** of your emotional programming.

Only **5%** of our emotional programming is formed during our **adult years**.

This means that the way our parents/guardians interact, show or don't show us love are the biggest influences on our choice of romantic relationships.

Some people are very fortunate to have been brought up by parents who exemplified a balanced, fulfilling and loving relationship. Most of us, however, have been emotionally programmed by less healthy relationship role models.

On top of this, we receive no guidance on how to form and maintain healthy relationships at school or otherwise. It is no wonder that we repeat destructive patterns emanating from emotional conditioning during the ages of 0-18.

If you are fortunate to have had good parental relationship role models, you'll read other reasons which explain why you may be repeating destructive relationship patterns.

The six steps to overcoming destructive relationship patterns

Step 1: Gain **awareness** of your relationship patterns

Step 2: Understand why you are repeating these patterns

Step 3: Identify the **warning signals** of your destructive patterns

Step 4: Create an image of a **healthy relationship** for yourself

Step 5: Build your **self-esteem**

Step 6: Say **no!**

Step 1:
Gain awareness of your relationship patterns

Read the following most common destructive relationship patterns and see if you have or are attracting this type of relationship into your life.

#1 Unavailable pattern

You have or are attracting partners who cannot commit to you fully since they:
- Are married or taken
- Live far away
- Are workaholics
- Have time-consuming hobbies or interests
- Have time-consuming family commitments
- Are emotionally unavailable

> **Candy's story**
>
> I repeated this pattern over and over again until I met my now husband. I started at the age of 17 with my first love, who was already taken.
>
> I then chose relationships with men who lived abroad. I realized this wasn't working and then fell in love with a man with a fiancée and young baby. At the time, I knew this was wrong but didn't seem to be able to stop myself. After much pain and hurt, I finally summoned up the courage to end this relationship.
>
> I then made it a rule not to date anyone who was attached but continued my unavailable pattern in different ways. I fell head over heels with a man who had so many family and work commitments that he barely had time for himself, let alone me. There were other men along the way who were unable to communicate and share their feelings, making them emotionally unavailable to me.

Why I repeated this pattern

There are two reasons why I kept repeating this pattern in different forms. Firstly, when I was growing up my mother was distant and showed little warmth or love so my brain equated love with being emotionally unavailable. When I met partners who were unavailable in some way, it felt familiar and comfortable, even though it didn't ultimately make me happy.

Secondly, I had a great fear of intimacy and showing any vulnerability. If I kept attracting unavailable types, I didn't have to get to an intimate stage and show any of my vulnerability, so being in unavailable relationships was a way of protecting myself.

Why you might be repeating this pattern

- As a child, love didn't seem available from one or both of your parents or other relatives.
- As a child, a parent or other relative abandoned you.
- As a child, a parent or other close relative died.
- Unavailable relationships stop you from having to show your vulnerability and getting hurt.

#2 Superficial pattern

You have or are attracted to superficial qualities in a potential partner such as looks, sexual attraction, money or social status over more important qualities such as honesty, reliability or good conversation.

> ### Amanda's story
>
> Amanda was attracted to DJs whom she met in bars and clubs. It didn't matter what they looked like, the draw of someone taking control behind the decks was enough to make her go weak at the knees. She kept imagining that as DJs, they would be sexy, great dancers, good in bed, interesting and the life and soul of a party. She was continually disappointed when they didn't live up to her expectations and could be introverted or more interested in themselves than her, unreliable and unable to commit.
>
> ### Why Amanda repeated this pattern
>
> Amanda repeated this pattern because she wasn't clear and wasn't being honest about what she really wanted in a relationship, e.g. good conversation, someone interested in her and someone whom she could rely on. She made the mistake of taking one superficial thing she was attracted to, a man DJing, and projecting her own ideas on to how those men should be without getting to know them first.

Why you might be repeating this pattern

- You're not clear about what you really want in a relationship.
- You're not being honest about what you really want in a relationship.
- You're not ready to get close to someone, so subconsciously you attract partners whom you know you will only have a superficial interest in.

#3 Best mate pattern

You have or are attracting men/women who seem to show you a lot of attention but don't want to take the relationship any further than friendship.

Hilary's story

Hilary met Tom and they seemed to have so much in common, enjoying the outdoors, film, stimulating conversation and cooking together. Tom was tall, dark and handsome, oozed testosterone and Hilary fancied the pants off him. They started to spend more and more time together, spoke on the phone every day and for Hilary the deep conversations and shared common interests made her feel very close to Tom.

Hilary started to wonder why Tom wasn't making any romantic advances towards her and thought that maybe he was taking it slowly. After three months, Hilary realized that Tom wasn't going to make the move so expressed her romantic interests. Hilary was devastated when Tom said that he wasn't interested in her that way and wanted to just be friends. Hilary continued to challenge Tom to find out why, since she saw great potential in a romantic relationship between them. Under duress, Tom said that Hilary wasn't his type and wasn't girly and feminine enough.

Why Hilary repeated this pattern

You will read in more detail in **Chapter 5** that in order for romantic relationships to be healthy and fulfilling there needs to be a balance of feminine and masculine energy. In the above situation with Tom and Hilary, Tom had very masculine energy and to complement him in a relationship needed a woman with very feminine energy. After working with me, Hilary came to realize this and developed and communicated her feminine side with men. She also came to realize that Tom had been using her to fulfill his needs for intimacy and emotional closeness without showing any commitment to Hilary. After this, Hilary started to attract men who were interested in her romantically and, interestingly, were not as Alpha Male.

> I have also worked with male clients who keep attracting women who never want to take the relationship further than friends. These women are attracted to men with more masculine energy to complement their feminine energy.
>
> You'll read more in **Chapter 5** how the woman can take the masculine role in a relationship and this will work if she is complemented by a man who takes the feminine role.

Why you might be repeating this pattern

- You're not communicating the masculine or feminine essence that you are most comfortable with.
- You let partners take advantage of your giving nature.

#4 Rescue pattern

You have or are attracting men/women who need rescuing because they:
- Have mental health issues.
- Are suffering from childhood traumas which they have not resolved.
- Are financially unstable.
- Suffer from very low self-esteem.
- Have not recovered from the trauma of being in an abusive relationship.

John's story

John worked in the caring profession and had strong empathy and great skills in helping others. He attracted beautiful women who were highly insecure, had issues from their childhood and previous relationships and expressed their pain by treating John atrociously.

Throughout these relationships, John felt that he was walking on egg shells since the slightest thing would enrage these women. They were jealous of John spending time with anyone else apart from themselves.

They continually ended the relationship and then begged to come back, some even threatening suicide. They clearly did need rescuing but John was not the person to do this. They needed professional help. When John started working with me he had broken up from his previous girlfriend but was still supporting her emotionally and even lending her money. She continued to blow hot and cold with John. With my help, John realized that going into rescue mode with his girlfriends was draining him of energy and not helping either him or his girlfriends. He made a conscious decision to form more equal and healthy relationships.

> ### Why John repeated this pattern
>
> John was repeating this pattern because he had grown up rescuing his brothers and sisters. He was the eldest of five and when his father left he took on the role of looking after his siblings at an early age. He had learnt a construct that love meant rescuing people in need. Once John realized this and that healthy and fulfilling relationships need to be formed on equal terms, he started to attract and settle down with more of an equal who cared for him as much as he cared for her.

Why you might be repeating this pattern

- You rescued a family member in your childhood so believe that love equals rescuing.
- You didn't succeed in rescuing a family member, such as a parent with mental health problems or addictions, so seek out a partner to rescue since you feel you have unfinished business to do.
- Rescuing gives you control in a relationship since you are the stronger party and stops you from getting hurt by someone stronger than you.

#5 Drama pattern

You have or are attracting men/women who bring a lot of drama into the relationship. Signs of drama in a relationship are:

- Lots of break-ups and passionate make-ups.
- Lots of anger and arguments.
- Shouting and screaming.

Kevin's story

Kevin thought that women who were calm, happy in themselves and generally grounded were boring. He enjoyed the unpredictability of women who argued with him, had mood swings from high to low, with whom he never quite knew where he stood. After a few years, these type of relationships took their toll on Kevin and he was putting so much energy into his relationships that he didn't have any to spend on his work, family, friends or health. He knew that he needed to break this addiction.

Why Kevin repeated this pattern

Kevin repeated this pattern because he was using his relationships to fulfill his need for variety.

Anthony Robbins, bestselling author and peak performance consultant identified that we have six basic needs which we all need to be fulfilled in some way. These needs are:

Certainty – the need to feel secure.

Uncertainty – the need for surprise, difference and change.

Significance – the need to feel you are good at something and stand out from others.

Love and connection – the need for intimacy and to share.

Growth – the need to grow and develop intellectually, emotionally and spiritually.

Contribution – the need to give back, help and nurture.

> We can choose either positive or negative "vehicles" to fulfill these needs. Kevin was using a negative vehicle and one which caused him a lot of pain to fulfill his need for variety. After working with me Kevin decided that a more stable, loving relationship would better serve him to fulfill his dreams and goals. He found other ways to fulfill his need for variety inside and outside of a relationship such as taking risks in his career and bringing spontaneity to his relationships in the form of romantic gestures.
>
> As well as attracting partners who bring drama to your relationship, you can be the one creating drama in your relationship. If you are creating drama in your relationship, you need to find different ways to fulfill your need for variety.

Why you might be repeating this pattern

- You believe that drama is the only way to fulfill your need for variety in a relationship or in your life as a whole.
- You feel insecure and unworthy in your relationship so you constantly sabotage it with dramatic behavior such as mood swings, attacks of jealousy and bouts of insecurity.

#6 I believe I can change them pattern

You have or are attracting men/women who you think you can change and then they will be perfect for you. These men/women may be:

- Unemployed or in a job they hate.
- Display unacceptable behavior such as cheating on you or abusing you physically, mentally or emotionally.
- Unable to commit due to intimacy issues.
- Impotent or have a low sex drive.

Kate's story

Kate met men who seemed to have great potential. They were intelligent, kind, good around her friends and family and seemed to dote on her at the beginning. The similarity between all of them was that none of them had a stable or fulfilling job.

Kate didn't see this as a problem since she thought she would be the one to help them find their dream job. Kate applied herself to doing job searches on the Internet for her boyfriends, updating their CVs, trying to persuade them to attend courses and training and bolstering them financially.

No matter how hard she tried, these boyfriends stayed unemployed or in dead-end jobs, until Kate ended the relationships, when to Kate's dismay they started to get their lives together.

Why Kate repeated this pattern

Kate repeated this pattern since she felt in control in these relationships and her boyfriends didn't compete with or threaten her career success. She stopped repeating this pattern when she realized that her controlling behavior was pushing her boyfriends away since they ended up feeling emasculated and smothered. With this realization, she started to choose relationships with men whom she didn't need to change and whom she was in love with for how they were when she met them, not how they would be in the future.

#7 Give, give, give pattern

You are the one in the relationship who gives much more than the other person. This can include:
- Paying for things and providing financial support.
- Showing more physical affection.
- Initiating and giving more during sex.
- Buying gifts.
- Listening and giving emotional support.

> ### Mary's story
> Mary was a very giving person inside and outside of her relationships. Giving may seem like the ultimate act of altruism but for Mary she gave to her detriment. She launched herself into relationships thinking that the more she gave the more the other person would give and love her. Very early on in her relationships, she would offer to pay for meals, theatre and concert tickets. As her relationships developed, she would take her boyfriends on expensive weekends away and luxurious holidays. Mary would spend hours listening to her partners' problems and spend time helping to resolve them. She would even initiate sex and give totally to her partner without receiving much back. Instead of loving and giving back, her partners got used to this treatment and took advantage of Mary's generosity. These partners lost respect for Mary since she didn't show much respect for herself and ended up treating her more and more badly until they left the relationship for someone else.

Why Mary repeated this pattern

Mary over-gave in her relationships because she had spent her whole life trying to win the affection of her father and equated love to having to prove herself through giving. Mary also didn't believe she was good enough to receive unconditionally so gave to make up for her lack of self-worth.

When Mary and I looked back over her past relationships, Mary realized that it was unhealthy for her to over-give and was harmful to the other person since they ended up taking advantage of Mary and treating her like a doormat. This was enough to inspire Mary to change.

She started by consciously giving less in her work and with her friends. Her friends were actually really pleased since they didn't like the way Mary ran herself ragged and became ill by giving and doing too much. Once Mary had begun to change her behavior with friends and at work, she felt confident that she would be able transfer this behavior into romantic relationships. She did! Now she is happily married to a man who will do anything for her and appreciates her for who she is rather than what she gives.

Why you might be repeating this pattern

- You don't believe you are worthy of someone loving and giving to you so you choose partners who prove this.
- You didn't feel loved as a child and constantly had to make people love you so you are continuing this pattern.
- You saw one of your parents being the giver and the other the taker so you are copying this relationship example.

#8 Take, take, take pattern

You are the one in the relationship who takes much more than the other person. This can include the other person:

- Paying for things and providing financial support.
- Showing you more physical affection.
- Giving more to you sexually.
- Buying you gifts.
- Listening and giving emotional support.
- Cooking, cleaning and washing for you.

Camilla's story

Camilla treated her boyfriends like doormats. These men drove her places, paid every time they went out, bought her expensive bunches of flowers, massaged her feet after a long day, cooked and cleaned for her, picked her and her friends up when they went on a girly night out and were an emotional rock for her.

Despite Camilla being treated like a princess in these relationships, she gradually lost respect for these men who didn't stand up to her and would do whatever she said and left one for the next one.

Why Camilla repeated this pattern

Camilla's father abandoned her and her mother when she was a young child so she felt deeply unloved by the most important man in her life. She realized that she was subconsciously taking out her anger on her boyfriends and taking the unloving role her father had played. She had therapy to resolve the issues with her father and then had the strength to form more balanced and equal relationships.

Why you might be repeating this pattern

- You feel safe taking control in a relationship so attract someone who you can control.
- You saw one of your parents being the taker and the other the giver so you are copying this relationship example.
- You are taking out your anger of not feeling loved by a parent on your partners.

#9 Worship pattern

You attract partners who worship you or you choose partners to worship. Examples of worshipping include:
- Someone older or a father or mother figure.
- Someone who has more social status.
- Someone who is renowned professionally.
- A teacher or professor.
- Someone who has a lot of power, such as a politician.
- Someone who is an entertainer, such as an actor/actress, singer, dancer, DJ or comedian.

> ### Steven's story
>
> Steven played in a band and frequently had girls coming up to him after gigs interested in getting to know him. He was flattered by the attention from girls 10 years his junior and attracted to their youthful energy and fresh faces. These young girls worshipped Steven and thought that everything that Steven was into was cool. They looked up to him as a role model and also as a father figure. Initially Steven reveled in the adulation but then became bored of spending time with girls who were far from being his equal and whom he felt he had to father. As these girls grew more confident and started to grow, they got tired of being treated as inferior to Steven. It was too late since the relationships were set up as unequal ones.

Why Steven repeated this pattern

Steven was not completely happy in himself and needed confirmation from his girlfriends that he was something special. He was also not happy growing older and younger women made him feel better about his age. Steven's last young worshipper ended up feeling resentful of Steven's superiority and control in the relationship and left him for another man. Steven was deeply hurt and realized that he needed to break this pattern and form more equal relationships. A few years later after getting his life together and feeling much happier, he met a slightly older woman who was secure in herself and his equal.

Why you might be repeating this pattern

- You worship partners because you don't feel special in yourself and need someone else to look up to.
- You attract partners who worship you because you don't feel secure in yourself and need adulation to affirm yourself.
- You didn't have a father or mother figure as a child and so seek this out in romantic partners.

Step 2:
Understand why you are repeating these patterns

You may have identified with one or several of the nine destructive relationship patterns. Identifying your patterns is the first step in letting go of them and going on to form healthy, equal and fulfilling relationships.

Once you have identified your pattern or patterns it is really helpful to understand the causes of these patterns. Knowing the causes can help you realize that you need some professional help, such as counseling or coaching to resolve these issues. Email me at

info@howtomeetyourperfectmatch.com

for more information on my coaching to break destructive relationship patterns. I can also assess whether you might be better suited to receiving counseling or therapy.

You may have already worked out why you are repeating your patterns by reading the nine examples. If you are still not sure as to why you are repeating your patterns, the following exercise can help you identify the programming up until the age of 18 which has affected your attitudes towards and choices in romantic relationships.

Exercise 1 – Awareness of how your conditioning has affected your choice in relationships

1. Write down any events or behavior during your childhood or adolescence which hurt you in some way in the first column of the table on **page 24,** for example:

- Parents separating.
- Loss of close family or friend.
- A sibling being favored over you.
- Physical, emotional or sexual abuse.
- Moving frequently and being separated from loved ones.
- Parents fighting.
- Absence of one or more parent figures.
- Being bullied or teased at school.
- Suffering from a long-term illness or health condition.
- Introduction of a step-parent into your life.
- Being constantly undermined by a parent or relative.

2. In the second column, write down how this event made you feel, for example, angry, sad or ashamed.

3. In the third column, write the belief that you created in response to this feeling, for example, I don't believe I'm good enough, I believe I have to work at being loved.

4. Select which of the 10 destructive relationship patterns you think you are repeating as a result of this belief.

Before you fill in your own table, there are some real-life examples on the next page from people I know and have worked with to help you create yours:

AWARENESS OF HOW YOUR CONDITIONING HAS AFFECTED YOUR CHOICE IN RELATIONSHIPS

Event/behavior	How this made me feel	The belief I created in response to this feeling	The type of relationship I attract as a consequence of this belief
One of sisters got attention from my parents for being pretty and the other for being intelligent	I felt unloved and unattractive	I believe I'm not attractive or clever enough to get a man's full attention	Unavailable type
My father left my mother and I when I was very young	I felt abandoned and unloved	I believe that no man I have a relationship with will stick around for me	Unavailable type
My father never showed me affection or praise	I felt that nothing I did would please my father	I believe that you have to prove your love to someone	Give, Give, Give type

AWARENESS OF HOW YOUR CONDITIONING HAS AFFECTED YOUR CHOICE IN RELATIONSHIPS

Event/behaviour	How this made me feel	The belief I created in response to this feeling	The type of relationship I attract as a consequence of this belief

Step 3:
Identify the warning signals of your destructive patterns

Once you have identified why you are repeating destructive relationship patterns, you need to ensure that you don't fall into the trap of repeating them again.

Something that has worked well for me and my clients is to identify the warning signs of your destructive relationship and to step back whenever you see or witness one of these. The best way to do this is to identify the similarities in your most significant relationships. When I wanted to break my pattern of attracting unreliable, lying commitment-phobes, I noticed that they were all taller than average, obsessed about their appearance and were late for or changed times for dates at the last minute. These quickly became important warning signals for me to watch out for.

Exercise 2

Here is an example of one of my client's list of similarities in the men she chose:

How and where you met	Quite random - in a café, through friends, internet dating, Buddhist centre
Physical appearance	Not very attractive, didn't take care of themselves
Age	A bit older than me or same age
Profession	Mixed bag. None into social change, which is very important to me

Values	Never done any volunteering, very self-centered
Shared interests (which ones)	Addictions – drinking and smoking
Intelligence (superior/inferior/equal to you)	Inferior intelligence to me
Financial status and attitude towards giving (superior/inferior/equal to you)	Inferior financial status to me, I paid for most things
Passion/physical relationship (strong, not so strong)	Strong to begin with and then broke down quickly, not sustained
Core beliefs and attitudes towards life	Deluded, hurt other people and didn't take responsibility
How they treat you (fairly, with disrespect, indifferently)	Show attention and then become indifferent and don't explain why
How the relationship progressed (intense start and then fizzling out, slow build-up, intense and throwing yourselves into commitment such as living together, no commitment or progression over time)	Intense and then fizzles out
Family background	Difficult family backgrounds
Similarity to your mother/father	Uncommunicative like my father

Before doing this exercise, she hadn't realized that most of the men that she attracted hadn't been very attractive (in her eyes) or looked after themselves very well, had addictions, always asked her to pay for things, didn't take responsibility for their lives and came from difficult family backgrounds. Shortly before we did this exercise, Victoria had arranged to go on a date with someone new. She had her warning signals top of mind and was put off the guy the moment he asked her to buy him a drink. She was disciplined enough not to take it any further and stopped herself from repeating her rescue relationship pattern.

She then attracted a man with none of her warning signals. **Awareness** and **discipline** work.

You can try out Exercise 2 yourself:

How and where you met	
Physical appearance	
Age	
Profession	
Values	
Shared interests (which ones)	

Intelligence (superior/inferior/equal to you)	
Financial status and attitude towards giving (superior/inferior/equal to you)	
Passion/physical relationship (strong, not so strong)	
Core beliefs and attitudes towards life	
How they treat you (fairly, with disrespect, indifferently)	
How the relationship progressed (intense start and then fizzling out, slow build up, intense and throwing yourselves into commitment such as living together, no commitment or progression over time)	
Family background	
Similarity to your mother/father	

Step 4:
Create an image of a healthy relationship for yourself

If you have always been in unhealthy, unfulfilled and unequal relationships that have drained you of energy, it can be difficult to imagine what a healthy relationship looks and feels like.

It is vital that you get a clear image of a healthy relationship; otherwise, you risk not believing you can have it and slipping back into your old familiar patterns.

It is especially important to believe in a relationship which is totally different from your current relationship pattern. For example, if you attract unavailable types, see, hear and feel yourself with someone available to you on an emotional, physical and mental level. The more you can engage your senses in this process, the more real the type of relationship you want will feel to you.

You can strengthen your belief in attracting a healthy relationship if you have good relationship role models around you.

- Observe friends, family, colleagues and neighbors who have healthy relationships and identify what makes those relationships work, for example, the partners listening to each other, making time for themselves as well as each other, having fun together, standing by each other through tough times and accepting each other, warts and all.
- If you don't know anyone in healthy relationships, look at relationships in the public light which you admire.

Finally, practice seeing, hearing, feeling and even tasting and touching what it is like to be in this healthy relationship on a regular basis. You can do this by simply daydreaming about how wonderful it will be when you're in this relationship.

When I was single, I wanted to visualize being in a fulfilling relationship but found it impossible because I thought I had to be able to clearly see my future partner. I couldn't see my future partner in my mind's eye because I hadn't met him yet. For this exercise to work you don't need to see specifics, you can go into a relaxed state and just feel the feelings you would have in a healthy relationship or hear the beautiful, romantic things that your partner is saying to you.

If you find it impossible to see, hear or feel anything about a future relationship, you may be struggling to believe that you can or deserve to meet your perfect match. **Chapter 3** will help you to overcome this limiting belief.

Step 5:
Build your self-esteem

The better you feel about yourself, the more respect you will have for yourself and the less likely you will be to disrespect yourself and repeat your past destructive relationship patterns. Self-esteem needs to be built and maintained on a regular basis. On the next page are some ways to make you feel good about yourself.

Build your confidence

> The more confident we feel, the happier we feel. You can build confidence by stepping out of your comfort zone and trying new challenges or taking risks. These could include a new sport or hobby, smiling and talking to strangers, going on holiday on your own or dressing more glamorously.

Look after yourself

> Treat your body well and your body treats you well. When you exercise regularly and eat a balanced diet, you develop that healthy glow which gives you confidence and attracts attention. Eating and staying active also gives you more energy to look for that special someone.

Treat yourself regularly

> Treat yourself with gifts and indulgences such as a massage, hot bath or DVD and days out, just as you would treat a partner.

Switch off your inner critic

> The nagging voice in your head that tells you that

you're stupid, unattractive, fat and generally not good enough will eat away at your self-esteem. Would you ever speak to a best friend or loved one with such contempt? Notice every time you speak negatively to yourself and immediately counteract this with a positive thought. This could be something as simple as "I've done well to get through a busy day's work today."

Practice an attitude of gratitude

Show love for yourself by appreciating yourself on a daily basis. Just as we can take our partners for granted, we can also take ourselves for granted. Take time every night to acknowledge one or several things that you have accomplished or contributed during the day. This could be anything from taking the time to help someone with directions or sending a loved one a special text.

Relax

One of the most powerful and sometimes hardest ways to love ourselves is to take time out from other commitments and relax. A conscious form of relaxation such as meditation, listening to a relaxation CD, exercising, going for a walk or spending a day without an agenda eases stress and anxiety and allows us to be more at one with ourselves.

Do something you've been putting off for ages

When you put something off, you feel worse and more guilty about not doing it. This can lead to negative self talk such as "you're so lazy" or "you never finish things", and this negativity eats away at your self-esteem. You release energy and feel empowered when you do the filing which has been piling up for months, finish that DIY job or call that relative you've been meaning to for months.

Bring some joy into your life

You can get sucked up into the routine of life and forget to do the things that bring you true joy and make you laugh. Joyful activities include dancing, socializing with friends, seeing live comedy or going to see a funny film or spending time in nature.

Step 6:
Say no!

You've done really well to:
- Gain awareness of your relationship patterns
- Understand why you have been repeating these patterns
- Identify the warning signals of a destructive relationship
- Create your image of a healthy relationship
- Build your self-esteem

The last step is to make sure you say "no" to any potential partner who shows signs of drawing you back into one of your destructive relationship patterns.

If you find it difficult to say no because you fear hurting someone else's feelings, remember what you are saying "yes" to by saying no. You will be saying yes to the loving, healthy and fulfilling relationship which you deserve.

Chapter 2

Letting go of past relationships to make way for future ones

Ten signs you are holding on to a past relationship

1. You **compare** every man/woman you meet to one or more of your exes.
2. You are **pursuing** an ex boyfriend/girlfriend who has made it clear that they are no longer interested in you romantically.
3. You **romanticize** about one or more of your past relationships.
4. You **can't forgive** an ex for the way they have treated you.
5. You **can't forgive yourself** for the way you have treated an ex.
6. You still **rely on** one or more exes for emotional and/or practical help.
7. One or more of your exes **still relies on you** for emotional/practical help.
8. You believe that you **will never find the kind of relationship** you had with one of your exes.
9. You have **photos** of one or more of you exes out on display.
10. You cherish **keepsakes** from exes.

Holding on to past relationships can stop you from attracting a new relationship into your life. This is because psychologically you don't have the "space" for someone new when you are consumed with thoughts and feelings for an ex. If you do meet someone new, this relationship is doomed to failure since this new person will either not live up to your expectations, or not feel special or loved enough.

Three tough truths

Truth #1: You are **mistreating** your new partner if you continually compare them to your ex.

Truth #2: You are **cheating** on your new partner if you are still giving your ex practical or emotional support which your new partner is not involved in.

Truth #3: You are **denying** your new partner first place in your life if you treasure keepsakes and photos from exes.

How to let go of past relationships

Here are solutions to the ten signs that you are holding on to a past relationship:

Sign #1: You compare every man/woman you meet to one or more of your exes

If you hold one of your exes in such high esteem that no one else measures up to them, you need to do a reality check and recognize why the relationship would never have worked.

> **SUSAN'S STORY**
>
> Susan always attracted "nice guys" and had a pattern of finishing these relationships after a couple of years. She recognized that most of her boyfriends just weren't dynamic enough to match her drive and energy. There was one, however, that she felt she let slip away. William was a nice guy but also gutsy enough to challenge Susan. Whenever Susan met potentials she would automatically compare them to William. No man was as kind, creative and funny as William. I asked Susan the ultimate question. "If William was so perfect, why did you finish with him?" Susan didn't know why, just that she left him for a more exciting relationship which quickly fizzled out. I then got Susan to identify what she admired so much in William. It turned out that Susan and William shared three important core values: integrity, creativity, and drive and energy. (You can read more in **Chapter 4** why sharing core values with your partner is critical to the success of your relationship.) This begged the question why things didn't work out between Susan and William.
>
> To get a better understanding I asked Susan how William's life had panned out since they split up and how her life was now. William was in the same job, living in the same town, married with two children. In contrast Susan had moved to a big city and set up a highly successful business. What I helped Susan identify was that she still felt great affection for William because of the core values they shared, but the relationship would never have worked in the long term since they had completely different visions for the future; his settled doing the same thing, hers moving forward and growing. This realization helped Susan to move on and stop comparing potentials to William.

Each relationship is different so it may not be that your vision with your ex differed. What I can assure you of is that there will be reasons why your relationship would not have worked; otherwise you would still be together. If you are finding it hard to identify why the relationship would not have worked in the long term, get some honest feedback from friends or family or contact me,

info@howtomeetyourperfectmatch.com

for a consultation to find out why.

Sign #2: You are pursuing an ex boyfriend/girlfriend who has made it clear that they are no longer interested in you romantically

There are several reasons why you might not be able to take no for an answer and continue to pursue an ex:

- You didn't get full closure on the relationship and your ex hasn't explained clearly enough why they are no longer interested.
- You became unhealthily obsessed in the relationship and are finding it hard to think rationally.
- You became unhealthily addicted to passionate "ups" and "downs" in this relationship and believe that after this down there has to be another up.

Some more **tough truths:**

- We all have a right to say no.
- When someone says no they mean no.
- You can't make someone love you.
- As much as you think that you are perfect for each other, your ex can think that you are completely wrong for each other.
- Frequent phone calls, texts, emails and turning up at an ex's work or home can be interpreted as harassment.

If you continue to pursue an ex who is not interested, you will create a never-ending cycle of disappointment, hurt and even anger for yourself and your ex. If you are concerned about your behavior being unusually irrational and obsessive, seek professional help from a therapist or counselor.

Sign #3: You romanticize about one or more of your past relationships

When you romanticize about a past relationship, you need to be honest about how good it really was. You might be convincing yourself that you'll never meet anyone like this again. If you keep up that belief, it gives you a great excuse not to take the scary step of going out there and meeting new potentials.

> ### Janet's story
>
> Janet had an on/off relationship with David over three years. She was drawn to David's passion, intellectual mind and the excitement he brought to their sex life. Janet also loved the way that David socialized easily and could entertain people for hours with his funny stories. After several break-ups and make-ups, David eventually finished the relationship to go off with another younger woman with whom he had been having an affair. Janet remained blind to David's infidelity, selfishness, disrespect and unreliability, and romanticized his charisma and passion. Eventually, close friends persisted in drawing a not-so-pretty picture of David and Janet realized that she would never have been happy if she had stayed with him. Janet changed her choice in men and formed a long-term relationship with a less charismatic but more honest and compatible man.

The moral of this story is to be honest about the darker side of your "perfect" ex and whether you could live with this for the rest of your life.

Sign #4: You can't forgive an ex for the way they have treated you

For me, forgiveness is one of the highest virtues and is by no means an easy process. However hard it may be to forgive, the effects of not forgiving someone can have a far more detrimental effect on you than on the other person. When you blame or hold deep resentment towards an ex, you become overwhelmed with the toxic emotions of hatred and anger. On a daily basis your thoughts are consumed with negativity towards that person. You may experience tension in your neck, shoulders or back where these negative emotions are stored. You may find it difficult to concentrate on anything other than resentment and anger towards your ex.

When a relationship comes to an end, it is normal and healthy to go through the emotional grieving cycle: relief, shock, denial, anger, depression and acceptance. It is unhealthy, however, to stay in the anger phase for more than a few months.

If you have been abused emotionally, mentally, physically or sexually in a relationship, I advise seeking the professional help of a therapist or counselor.

If your ex behaved unfavorably or disrespectfully but not abusively, the below tips may help you to forgive him/her:

- When you forgive someone, you don't have to condone or accept the behavior which hurt you. For example, you can forgive someone for being unfaithful but this doesn't mean letting them be unfaithful to you again.
- Understand why your ex behaved in the way they did. For example, they may have shut you out and withdrawn emotionally towards the end of the relationship because they were unable to tell you how they were really feeling.

- The anger and resentment you are feeling towards your ex is hurting and consuming you more than them, unless you are actively seeking revenge.
- Your ex is probably feeling guilty and regretful about the way they treated you.
- Don't forgive too soon – it is important to experience the emotions of anger and regret.
- It is incredibly empowering to let the other person know that you have forgiven them – face to face, in writing or, if you are out of touch, imagine in your mind that you are telling them.
- We all make mistakes and hurt others, the important thing is that we learn from these mistakes and grow

For a further understanding of forgiveness and strategies to forgive:

Forgiveness: How to Make Peace with Your Past and Get on with Your Life by

— Sidney B Simon

Sign #5: You can't forgive yourself for the way you treated an ex

Not forgiving yourself can be more damaging than not forgiving an ex. When you direct blame, anger and resentment towards yourself, you are continually telling yourself what a bad person you are. This leads to diminishing self-esteem until you don't think you're worthy of anyone, let alone your perfect match. Here are some tips if you are finding it hard to forgive the way you behaved with an ex:

- You were a different, younger self when you behaved in the way you did.
- Acknowledge that you have learnt from your mistakes and wouldn't treat anyone like this again.
- It takes two to tango so consider what your ex did to allow or invite your behavior.
- Apologize to your ex face-to-face, in writing or, if you are out of touch, imagine in your mind that you are apologizing or write a letter which you never send.
- Get perspective from friends or family as to how bad your behavior really was and whether there was any justification for your behavior.

Signs #6 and #7: You still rely on one or more of your exes for emotional/practical help and/or one or more your exes still relies on you for emotional or practical help

If you and an ex are supporting each other practically or emotionally, you are still intimately connected. If you are still both single and happy with this arrangement then it can work. Problems arise, however, when one of you starts a new relationship and the new partner is not involved.

Be wary of being too dependent on an ex for help and mistaking this kindness for romantic interest in you. Also be wary of the ex who uses you for support since they don't have a partner in their life. You can misinterpret their need for help as a need for you romantically.

If you manage to integrate an ex into your life as a friend and new partners accept this, then there is no problem with continuing to be there for each other as friends. Be on alert if you are relying on your ex to do things or support you emotionally in a way that your current partner cannot or will not.

Sign #8: You believe that you will never find the kind of relationship/person you had with one of your exes.

This is another way of expressing signs #1 and #3 and the same advice applies to consider honestly whether your ex was all you crack them up to be.

Signs #9 and #10: You have photos of one or more of your exes on display and/or you cherish keepsakes from your exes

How would you feel if you walked into a new partner's house and saw a picture of one of their exes smiling back at you? This happened to me and I immediately thought: "Three's a crowd, I'm outta here." Even if you are still single, take down pictures of exes and put them away. Having pictures of exes out on display signals that you are not ready to move on and will drive potentials away.

It is fine to hold on to gifts from exes if you are keeping them for their practical use or aesthetic beauty, but not because they hold sentimental value. If you have kept emails, text messages, tickets from dates, notes and little gifts from exes, you are clearly holding on to the past and need to let go of these in order to move on and start a new relationship.

Chapter 3

Your perfect match – what's holding you back from meeting The One

From my experience of coaching hundreds of clients, the one thing that most holds single people back from meeting their perfect match is **lack of belief** that they are **able** and **will** meet that special someone.

Having rather than lacking belief is critical to success in all areas of your life. Consider what the world would be like if JK Rowling had **believed** the 200 publishers who said that her first Harry Potter book was rubbish. How different would the world be if Barack Obama had **believed** that he didn't have enough experience to become the first black president of America? What will your life be like if you carry on **believing** that you'll never meet your perfect match?

Common limiting beliefs about relationships

See if any of the below most common limiting beliefs about relationships resonate with you:

1. **Full diary/no time:** I believe I'm too busy to meet anyone.
2. **Fear of rejection:** I believe I will be rejected if I approach or get involved with anyone so it's not worth trying.

3. **Procrastination:** I believe that I'm quite happy as I am, I don't need to be married for another 5-10 years.
4. **Delay tactics**: I believe that I need to get my career sorted/lose weight/change jobs/move house before I commit to a relationship.
5. **Not good enough syndrome:** I believe that I'm too old to attract anyone, I'm not witty enough to chat anyone up, I'm too fat/skinny etc.
6. **False optimism:** I believe that I enjoy my single lifestyle, I can cope being alone better than others.
7. **False confidence:** I believe that I'm not that desperate – only desperate people actively look for someone.
8. **It's all over:** I believe that there are no decent guys out there – they're either players, gay or I don't fancy them. All the girls are too standoffish and impossible to talk to.
9. **Unrealistic wish list:** I believe that he has to be tall, dark and handsome, she's got to be fit, blonde and a great mother, he's got to earn 100k, she's got to do all the housework and look glamorous at all times.
10. **Living in the past:** I believe that I've been hurt so much that I can't put myself through that again.
11. **Miss Independence:** I believe that I don't need a man to do my DIY, carry my shopping, kill spiders or open doors for me.
12. **Mr Confirmed Bachelor:** I believe that I don't want a woman to disrupt my perfect single lifestyle of leaving washing up, eating take-outs in bed, playing as much Play Station as I want.

13. **Closed off to opportunities:** I believe that I don't have enough opportunities to meet anyone since I have a limited and established circle of friends.
14. **Not picking up on signals:** I believe that I can't pick up on encouraging signals.
15. **Best mate syndrome:** I believe that all the people I fancy want to be my best mate.
16. **Dark ages approach to flirting and dating:** I believe that the man always has to make the first move.
17. **Coming across as desperate:** I believe that I come across as desperate so put the opposite sex off.
18. **Addicted to con artists, aka Prince Charmings:** I believe that I can only attract good-looking, unreliable, superficial types.
19. **Trapped in unavailable patterns:** I believe that I can only attract men/women who are married, live far away or are too busy to spend much time with me.
20. **Not able to be alone:** I believe that I would rather be with anyone rather than no one, so choose the wrong type of relationships.

If you are holding one or more of the above beliefs then you will find it near impossible to meet your perfect match.

What is a belief?

A belief is a strong feeling of certainty about an idea. To have certainty about an idea, you need to back it up with proof or evidence. The more proof or evidence that you have, the stronger the belief becomes. So, if you believe that there are no decent men or women out there, you will have and will continue to collect evidence to support this. For example, you may try internet dating and meet a few unsuitable potentials and say: "See, I knew there were no decent men/women out there."

Empowering and limiting beliefs

Beliefs dictate how we feel about things and are empowering, limiting or neutral. If your ultimate dream is to meet your perfect match, a belief that there are no decent men/women will be limiting. Having such certainty will make it hard for you to recognize a decent guy even if he stares you in the face, because your belief has closed you off to the possibility of meeting the right person. A more empowering belief would be: "My perfect match is out there waiting for me." Having certainty in this belief would make you much more open to meeting potentials and trying new things.

The more certain and more fixed a belief becomes, the less likelihood there is of you challenging it or believing the opposite. This can work to your disadvantage if you hold a limiting belief such as "I'm not good enough" and to your advantage if you hold an empowering belief. Barack Obama became fixed and certain that he could win the American presidential elections of 2008 and this strong belief worked to his advantage.

How you can overcome your limiting beliefs

In order to overcome limiting beliefs stopping you from meeting your perfect match, you need to understand **why** you are investing so much energy in keeping these beliefs alive.

The primary reason that you are holding on to your limiting beliefs is because you are **scared**. Falling in love can be a frightening prospect.

You could get hurt again, make a fool of yourself or be rejected. Fear has its place when it stops us from doing something dangerous like rock climbing without safety equipment. Fear becomes debilitating when it stops us from striving for what we want.

There is also always a **benefit** to you for holding on to a limiting belief, otherwise you wouldn't hold on to it so tightly. Here are some examples:

Belief #1: "I believe that I can't pick up on encouraging signals from the opposite sex."

Benefit of this belief: If I believe that I can't pick up on encouraging signals from potentials, I don't have to put myself in situations where potentials may flirt or chat me up. The benefit to me is that by not putting myself in potential flirting situations, I can protect myself from getting hurt or being rejected.

Belief #2: "I believe that I can cope on my own and don't need a man/woman."

Benefit of this belief: I can stay in my comfort zone of remaining independent, doing what I want and not having to compromise and share.

> ### Melanie's story
>
> Melanie was a successful, attractive and confident woman in her 40s. She had a happy and rich life but lacked the fulfilling romantic relationship that she deserved. Melanie had had a few long-term relationships but none of them had truly worked. Melanie had a good understanding as to why her relationships had ended and wouldn't have worked in the long term and was ready to move on. When I first met Melanie, it was too painful for her to even think about being with a man yet deep down she really did want to meet her special someone and get married. She had a whole list of limiting beliefs which were stopping her from doing anything towards her goal of meeting her soul mate: "I can't meet a man with equal or greater intelligence than me", "I only attract emotionally unavailable men", "There is no way I can meet anyone on the internet", "I'm too old to get married." Melanie was resistant to thinking differently and shifting her beliefs because in her mind, she had so much evidence to back up these beliefs.
>
> Then there was a shift when I helped Melanie to realize that: "The reason I hold on to these beliefs is because they stop me from getting hurt."
>
> The more energy she put into these limiting beliefs, the more certain they became and the more protected she felt.
>
> Melanie was a brave and honest woman who knew that being with a loving, supportive husband was much more important to her than protecting herself from **maybe** getting hurt.
>
> At this point, Melanie spurred herself into action, redid her online profile and started going on dates.

> ### Nathalie's story
>
> Nathalie was driven, successful and in her late 30s and had no problems getting dates or forming relationships. Her relationships were never quite right and the men that she attracted didn't give her first place in their lives and were not willing to commit. She could feel her body clock ticking and wanted to settle down, get married and have children. Nathalie was working hard to improve her self-esteem so that she could attract the man she deserved. Nathalie was doing well and had built her confidence up but she admitted to me that there was one thought which kept going around in her head, "I'm going to end up with the wrong guy or single for the rest of my life." She knew that she had to overcome this belief in order to reach her goal of getting married and having children. I helped Nathalie to realize that her limiting belief was protecting her from getting hurt and stopping her from experiencing the pain of previous relationships. Nathalie had a breakthrough when I pointed out that she was putting more energy into avoiding pain than in attracting pleasure (getting married and having children). From this point, Nathalie realized that logically she had to put more energy into the pleasure she so wanted. She started to feel happier in herself and dating more suitable men.

Once you have identified why you are holding on to a limiting belief and the benefit of it, you need to replace it with a new, empowering one.

Examples include:

Old limiting belief	New empowering belief
I don't need a man	My life will be richer and more fulfilling with a man in it
I'm too busy to be in a relationship	I am creating space in my life for a relationship
I need to lose weight before I meet anyone	I am working towards my goal of losing weight and enjoying dating at the same time

Tip: It sends a powerful message to the subconscious mind if you write down your old, limiting belief on a piece of paper, say goodbye to it for the last time and then burn it. Obviously, burn your belief safely without causing a fire.

Exercise 3

Here is a process to help you let go of your limiting beliefs with a real-life example. You can then fill in your own version.

1. **Identify the limiting belief which you want to overcome**

    I want to overcome the belief that I'm not good enough to meet someone.

2. **What are the benefits of holding on to this belief?**

    (For example, staying in my comfort zone, maintaining my independence, not getting hurt, not losing face, etc)

    If I carry on believing that I am not good enough, I won't attract any potentials and without any potentials, there is no danger that I will be rejected again for not being good enough.

3. **What will my life be like in 5 and 10 years' time if I don't let go of this belief?**

   If I carry on believing that I am not good enough, in 5-10 years time I will be old and lonely, living in an apartment surrounded by cats. All of my friends will be married with children; I will be the odd one out at parties and weddings. I will be feeling sad and lonely on Saturday nights when there is no one else to go out with.

   What will my life be like in 5 and 10 years times if I let go of this belief right now? If I let go of this belief right now, I will have met my perfect match in 5 years time and we will be building our life together, making each other laugh, supporting each other through the highs and lows of life and making each other happy.

4. **What can I challenge about this belief (why is it not true/ridiculous)?**

   It is ridiculous to think that I am not good enough since my friends think of me as loving, kind and caring. I am fit and healthy and take care of my appearance.

5. **Why MUST I let go of this belief?**

   I have to let go of this belief so that I can move on in my life and have the relationship that I truly deserve. Also, my friends and family are tired of me saying, I'm not good enough and tired of seeing me complaining about being single but doing nothing about it.

6. **What is my new belief to replace this belief?**

   "I am not good enough to meet someone
   To
   "I am attractive, funny, intelligent and a good catch."

Exercise 4 – Reinforcing new and empowering beliefs

Creating a new and empowering belief, such as "I am attractive, funny, intelligent and a good catch", is an important step. However, this belief is a long way from your previous thinking of "I'm not good enough to meet someone." In order to bridge the gap between what you **believed** and what you now **want to believe**, you need to convince yourself that the new belief is true.

The way we form our beliefs can be thought of as a table. A table is made up of a table top and legs. Without the legs, the table top would fall down. In the same way as a table top is supported by table legs, a belief (the table top) is held up by references (table legs).

Let's take the limiting belief example "I'm not good enough". If this is a strong belief for you, there will have been things people have said, situations you have been in and things you have done to keep this belief alive. These are the table legs. Here is a visual example:

In order to smash this belief and believe in the new one ("I am attractive, funny and a good catch"), you need to create a new empowering belief (table top) and new references (legs) to support it.

Here is an example:

Empowering belief: "I'm attractive, funny and a good catch"

Reference: A man stopped me in the street to say how much he liked my dress

Reference: I often get attention from men when I go out.

Reference: I make everyone laugh at work and colleagues miss my sense of humor when I am off sick or on holiday.

To make your new empowering belief more powerful than the old limiting one, you need to keep collecting references which prove it. You can ask family and friends why they think it's true and put yourself in situations where your belief can be proved.

Exercise 4: Your examples

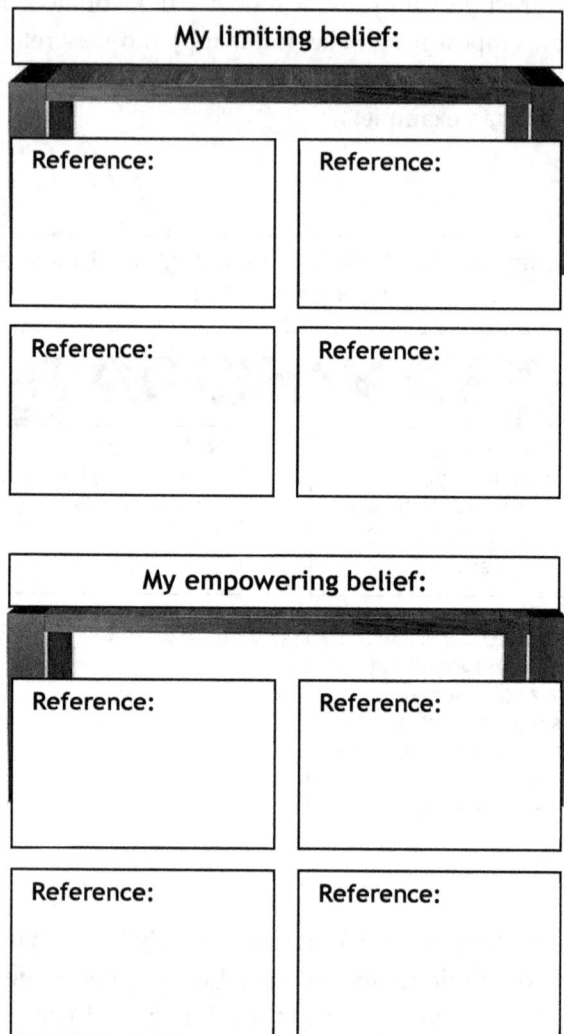

Overcoming your limiting beliefs about yourself and relationships is critical to your success in meeting your perfect match. Be honest about which limiting beliefs you are holding and use Exercises 3 and 4 to create new empowering ones.

Chapter 4

How to get the relationship you want

"We don't wait around for a fulfilling job, new house or even a new pair of shoes to land in our laps so why do we sit at home waiting for Mr or Mrs Right?"

— Candy Jannetta

Anything in life is hard to achieve if you're not clear enough about what you want. This is why countless books are written and bought on goal-setting and why businesses invest time and energy into setting and reviewing short and long-term objectives. You wouldn't buy a house or apartment without considering your budget, how many bedrooms you want, whether you need a garden or not, location, style or whether it needs renovation. Yet I've met hundreds of business-minded, successful singles who cling on to the old myth:

"I'll know my perfect match when I meet them"

I then answer:

"If you don't ask for what you want, you are not likely to get it."

The more specific you can be about the type of person and relationship you want, the easier your quest for Mr/Mrs Right will be.

Being certain about and communicating what you want will also help attract a long-lasting rather than short-lived relationship.

This chapter will give you the tools to outline exactly what you want in a long-term partner.

Why you need to know what you want in a relationship

- If you identify and focus on what you do want, you are less likely to attract what you don't want.
- When you know what type of person you are looking for, you are less likely to dismiss potentials who could be right for you.
- Knowing what you want will help you to write a more compelling online profile.
- Knowing what you want and telling others will help them to look out for suitable potentials for you.
- Knowing the type of person you are looking for gives you more clues as to where you might meet/find them.
- Getting clear about what you want in a relationship helps you to focus on the important rather than superficial things in potentials.

The four problems with making a list

You may have written lists of what you wanted in a potential partner/relationship in the past. I know that these lists haven't worked, otherwise you wouldn't be reading this book.

Before developing **Exercise 5**, I too wrote lists about the type of person I wanted to be with. There were four problems with my lists:

Problem #1: I wasn't **specific enough** about what I wanted, so I asked for general qualities like a good sense of humor without realizing that I needed to state the type of humor I was looking for, for example, dry and witty since overly sarcastic humor winds me up.

Problem #2: I focused too much on what I didn't want rather than what I did want. Remember that if you focus too much on what you don't want in life that is exactly what you will get.

Problem #3: My lists were too black and white and didn't show any compromises on my part.

Problem #4: Because other people said that I was being too fussy, I stopped writing down what I ideally wanted in a relationship and tried to be "realistic".

After identifying these four problems, I created a tool to overcome them. After using this tool, countless clients have emailed me to say that the partner that they have met has almost exactly matched the list they made.

> ### Rachel's story
> Dear Candy,
>
> I met my new partner Matt over a year ago at a retreat and we both went to the same retreat again in October. We got together as a couple then and we have been together ever since. He's now moving in with me! I read my list from your first workshop the other week and he ticked most of the boxes, with the exception of owns his own flat and is earning at least the same as I am. But he has ticked the spirituality box, the warm and loving and intimate box, and he is comfortable with himself box. He also fitted the 27-33 years old box – yes he's four years younger than me! He wants marriage and children even though he's only 33. So I'm very, very happy and I just wanted to say thank you for two wonderful workshops. I wish you every success in your business :)
>
> Rachel x

How to identify what you want

There are three steps in this process:

1. You write down your **ideal** in a relationship under the 13 categories. These are the qualities and behaviors that you dream of, not the ones which you think you can realistically attract. It is important to write down your ideal since you may well attract your ideal in some of the categories and you don't want to let go of high standards, just because friends and family say that "you are being too fussy".

2. You write down what you **cannot tolerate** in a relationship under the 13 categories. You need to be very honest with yourself and admit what you have tolerated in past relationships and are now not willing to accept. Although you don't want to focus too much on what you **cannot tolerate** you need to get this down on paper to pre-

vent you from making past mistakes and attracting destructive relationships.
3. You write down what you **can tolerate** in a relationship under the 13 categories. This is the most difficult section to fill in. It is very important to identify aspects that you can tolerate in a relationship since if you just focus on your **ideal** and **cannot tolerate**, you will be pushing away a lot of potential partners who could make you very happy. None of us are perfect so we are unlikely to meet someone who ticks all of our **ideal** boxes.

It is far better to be open to tolerating and compromising on some areas in a relationship. Don't forget that your perfect match will also be tolerating some of your behaviors, beliefs and personality traits. The best way to identify what you can tolerate in a relationship is to go through your **ideal** lists and see if there are any points which are not so important to you or you could live without. You might also find that there are some **cannot tolerates** that you could indeed tolerate. Be careful, though, not to compromise on important **cannot tolerates.**

Before you complete your own process, here is an example using the intellectual and practical intelligence category:

1. Intellectual and practical intelligence (academic, current affairs, arts, mental agility, political awareness, specific skills such as DIY, cooking, organizational, driving)

Ideal	Can tolerate	Cannot tolerate
<ul><li>Bright, curious, questioning</li><li>Into reading the same books as me</li><li>Loves learning</li><li>Knowledgeable about current affairs and politics</li><li>Very practical</li><li>Good at DIY</li></ul>	Reads a breadth of books Not so interested in current affairs and politics Basic level of DIY	Real academic who talks down to you Someone who isn't at all ambitious Someone who is totally impractical Someone who is not into cooking at all

Exercise 5 – for you to complete

1. Intellectual and practical intelligence (academic, current affairs, arts, mental agility, political awareness, specific skills such as DIY, cooking, organizational, driving)

Ideal   **Can tolerate**   **Cannot tolerate**

2. Emotional intelligence (intuition, ability to communicate their feelings, supportive, empathy, high self-awareness, common sense, creativity)

Ideal   **Can tolerate**   **Cannot tolerate**

3. Behavior (fidelity/infidelity, verbal/psychological/physical abuse, punctuality, reliability, embraces friends of same and opposite sex, willing to spend time with my family, personal hygiene)

Ideal   **Can tolerate**   **Cannot tolerate**

4. Fundamental beliefs (religious/spiritual, political, racial, sexual orientation, human and animal rights, disability, corporal punishment, environment, positive thinking, respect for self and others, abortion, put family first)

    Ideal   **Can tolerate**   **Cannot tolerate**

5. Location (same area, city, country, living arrangements)

    Ideal   **Can tolerate**   **Cannot tolerate**

6. Interests (sports, culture, travel, walking, bars and restaurants, reading etc).

    Ideal   **Can tolerate**   **Cannot tolerate**

7. Physical appearance (height, weight, body shape, facial features, hair, clothes and grooming, facial hair, posture, skin complexion, nationality/race)

    Ideal   **Can tolerate**   **Cannot tolerate**

8. Humor (sarcasm, dry, silly, childish, clever)

    Ideal   **Can tolerate**   **Cannot tolerate**

9. Which type of roles are most important for your perfect match to play in your life? (Father/mother, lover, friend, playmate, companion, partner, sister/brother)

    Ideal   **Can tolerate**   **Cannot tolerate**

10. Attitudes to physical, mental and emotional health (values fitness, enjoys/doesn't enjoy smoking, alcohol, drugs, emotionally aware, takes time out for themselves)

Ideal **Can tolerate** **Cannot tolerate**

11. Financial status (financially stable, equal status, has more money, happy to support someone else, etc)

Ideal **Can tolerate** **Cannot tolerate**

12. Age (preference for younger. older, similar age)

Ideal **Can tolerate** **Cannot tolerate**

13. Physical relationship (sexual preferences, frequency, physical affection etc)

Ideal	Can tolerate	Cannot tolerate

Now you have completed Exercise 5, consider these key points:
- You can only turn down men/women with **cannot tolerate** characteristics.
- Reflect on how many **cannot tolerate** characteristics there were in your past relationships.
- Reflect on relationships you have ended because of **can tolerates.**

Core values – their importance and how they impact on your relationships

Your core values are your rules for life and influence the relationships you form, the career you choose, the place you live and the interests you pursue. Your core values underpin your beliefs and your behaviors. Your values are developed at a subconscious level, coming from your family, friends, religious or spiritual teaching, teachers, peers and colleagues. Values can change over time, as you change. However, there will usually be about three values that remain constant throughout your life.

Your values are so integral and important to you that when you go against them, you can feel an enormous amount of stress.

> ### Tom's story
>
> I worked with a client called Tom who had been unhappy and stressed in his job as an art director for over a year. He couldn't understand why he was feeling this way since he loved what he did and worked for a good company. After we worked out Tom's core values, I asked him how these were fulfilled in his job. Tom's values of creativity, energy, fun and security were very well fulfilled at work. It was a different story when I asked Tom how his top value – integrity –was fulfilled at work. He realized that his integrity was continually being compromised since he was under pressure from his boss to lie to prospective clients in order to generate new business. Tom loved doing the work for clients but hated the disappointment and distrust generated when he and his team couldn't deliver on what was originally promised. Tom ended up changing jobs to a smaller, less prestigious design company where he was able to be more honest with his clients.

Core values are individual and it doesn't matter what yours are, so long as you choose a lifestyle where they can be honored.

One of the key signs of a healthy relationship is one where the two partners share, not all, but three to four core values. A couple who share core values will build their relationship around these. My husband and I share the core values of love, integrity and health. We manage to limit conflict in our relationship by living our core values in the following ways:

- We prioritize family and friends over work so honor our shared value of love.
- Sticking to our word and speaking honestly is paramount to our relationship so we honor our shared value of integrity.
- We invest time to stay physically fit and enjoy healthy food so honor our shared value of health.

A relationship feels right when you share core values. A relationship feels wrong and difficult when your values conflict with those of your partner.

Exercise 6 – discovering your core values

You can discover your core values by following the process below. It can be helpful to do this with a trusted friend.

1. What and who is important to you in your life? (For example: family, friends, my children, my dog, my job, my home, exercise, politics, reading, gardening, music, film, theatre, sports, etc).

2. Once you have a list of what and who is important to you in your life, ask yourself: What does this give me? And/or: Why is this important to me?

Here are some examples:

What/who is important to me in my life?	What does it/they give me? Why is this important to me?
Family	Love, support, affection, connection, fun They are there when I need them
My job	Fulfillment, achievement, security I'm able to be creative,
My home	Security, sense of well-being, peace and tranquility I love relaxing in my garden
Music	Fun, expression, good to dance to It lifts my mood
Adrenaline sports	Adventure, surprise, high energy It gives me a buzz

1. From both questions 1 and 2, pull out key words which you think are values. Here are some from the above example: love, support, affection, fun, connection, fulfillment, achievement, creativity, security, peace and tranquility, fun, adventure, energy.

2. Notice any words which have a similar meaning or go together, for example: love, support, affection and connection. Choose one word to group these similar words together, such as love.

3. You should end up with 7-10 core values. If you have more than 10, look out for any similarities or any which aren't as important to you so probably aren't core values.

4. You now have an idea of your core values. Don't forget that these can change over time and it is worth repeating the exercise on a yearly basis.

Why having a shared vision is so important

Do you remember Susan's story in **Chapter 2**? She couldn't let go of her past relationship with William because they shared core values. She realized, however, that the relationship wouldn't have worked in the long term since they had completely different visions for the future.

Before you meet your perfect match, you need to be clear about your vision for the future and the part you want him/her to play in that. Here are some questions to help you identify your vision for the next five years. You need to be honest about these and get clarity on any which you answer with "don't know" or "not sure".

Exercise 7 – clarifying your vision for the next five years

- Do you want to get married in the next five years?
- Do you want to have children in the next five years?
- Where do you want to live in the next five years?
- Where would you like to travel to in the next five years?
- How do you want your career to progress in the next five years?
- What interests or pursuits do you want to take up in the next five years?
- Which dreams do you need to fulfill in the next five years?
- Which health goals do you have for the next five years?
- Which financial goals do you have for the next five years?

If your partner has a very different vision of the next five years, for example, you want to get married and have children and they want to sell up and travel around the world, your relationship is destined for failure. To ensure the long-term success of a relationship, both partners need to be travelling in a similar direction and supporting each other along the way.

After doing Exercises 6 and 7 with me, clients often ask two questions:

- How am I going to ensure that I don't get charmed by a date and attract the same Mr/Mrs Wrongs who I've attracted in the past?
- When should I find out if my date is a perfect match?

How to ensure you don't attract another Mr or Mrs Wrong

When you meet someone who is not interested in a long-term relationship or not interested in a serious relationship with you, their behavior during the first phase of dating will give this away. Here are some tell-tale signs that a date is either not interested in long-term commitment or not interested in a long-term commitment with you:

- Your date turns up late and has feeble excuses.
- Your date cancels at the last minute.
- Your date only wants to see you during the week and not at weekends.
- Your date is secretive about where they live, what they do, who their friends are and any other basic information.
- Your date doesn't phone when they say they will.
- Your date wants you to come round to their house rather than take you out.

- Your date is reluctant to introduce you to their friends.
- Your date is reluctant to meet your friends.
- Your date has long telephone conversations while out with you.
- Your date is hard to get hold of and doesn't return phone calls or texts.
- Your date is not attentive to how you look, what you have to say or how you are feeling.
- Your date doesn't have much money and wants you to pay for everything.
- Your date doesn't make much effort in the way they dress and groom themselves when they see you.
- Your date shows disrespect towards something that is important to you such as, your work, children, beliefs, interests, etc.
- Your date visits you for sex and leaves without staying the night.

If you experience any of the above, it doesn't matter how good the chemistry is between you or how interesting you find your date, this relationship is not going to work in the long term.

When you should discover if your date is a potential perfect match

This is a bit like asking how long is a piece of string? But it is a very important point to consider. If you experience any of the above behavior, there should be no doubts in your mind that this person is not your perfect match. If, however, they are not obviously showing any of these behaviors, you need to search deeper. If you have been disappointed in the past, you don't want to invest too much time in a relationship which is not going anywhere or is going to leave you feeling hurt or rejected after an abrupt ending. There are a few assumptions that you need to make in order to make a decision as to when you need to work out if this is the right relationship for you:

Assumption #1: When you meet partners who are 35 years old or over, they usually have a better idea of what they want in a relationship based on past experience.

Assumption #2: When you form relationships at the age of 35 or over, you usually have a better idea of what you want in a relationship based on past experience.

Assumption #3: When you are direct with partners, they are usually honest about what they want in a relationship.

If you feel comfortable about making these assumptions about you and your partner, you can start thinking about the best time to work out whether your partner is worth investing in and could be your perfect match.

If you are enjoying your partner's company, the relationship seems to be flowing, you feel excited to see them every time you go on a date, these are signs that your relationship is worth continuing. However, make sure you live in the moment during the first stage of the relationship (as much as you possibly can), usually around two to three months, to find out about and enjoy each other before rushing to think and plan for the future. If, after two to three months the relationship seems to be progressing, you are still feeling excited and you can't wait to spend more time with your partner then it is time to start asking whether your partner could be the one for you. Read the next section for some specific ways of finding out if your date is a potential perfect match.

How you can work out if your date is a potential perfect match

You've done the hard work by identifying your ideal, can tolerates and cannot tolerates, discovering your core values and getting clear about your vision of the future.

You now need the tools to find out whether your date has any cannot tolerates or ideals, if they share any of your core values and if they have a similar vision of the future to you.

How to identify cannot tolerates and ideals in my partner

There are certain categories that are easier to identify than others.

Location

You will probably know this before you meet your date. It is worth asking early on in the relationship about how happy they are living where they are and if they have any future plans to move.

Interests

It is easy to ask your date about what they do in their free time and even go on some dates where you participate in each others' interests.

Physical appearance

You will obviously see this when you meet. Be wary of dismissing someone too quickly over how they look since it is the chemistry you have with someone rather than specifically how they look which attracts you to them.

Humor

You should be able to quickly pick this up during conversations.

Attitudes to physical, emotional and mental health

You should be able to find out pretty quickly whether someone smokes or drinks heavily or not at all. You can also find out easily whether someone does any physical exercise. You can find out how much a date takes care of themselves by listening out for what they do for themselves in their spare time. It may be harder to find out about someone's occasional drug use.

Age

You need to have a certain amount of trust that your date is telling the truth about their age.

Physical relationship

This needs to be tested once you feel enough trust to embark on it.

The remaining categories are not so immediately obvious so here are some questions you can ask to get a better idea.

Intellectual and practical intelligence

This can be assessed through conversation, the type of job someone has and their interests. In terms of practical intelligence, you can ask them about their home and get an idea about what they do around the house, such as DIY or cooking.

Behavior

This is a key area and the hardest to assess. There are behaviors which you can look out for, such as punctuality and reliability. It is harder to find out whether someone will be faithful, be open to your family and friends, caring towards your children and generally non-abusive. There are, however, some clues to someone being decent, thoughtful and caring. Someone who spends time doing thoughtful things for their friends and family is more likely to do thoughtful things for you. Someone who has a close and trusting relationship with their children is more likely to be able to build a close and trusting relationship with you. Someone who does volunteering, community work or things for others is more likely to be generous towards you. Someone who is loyal to friends and family is more likely to be loyal to you.

Fundamental beliefs

Someone who has very strong beliefs is more likely to express them early on. If you have strong beliefs that are important to you, such as spiritual, religious or political, you can express them and gauge your date's reaction to them.

Roles that your perfect match will play in your life

I would advise against asking your date whether they want to be a mother or father to your children or your husband or wife until you are more established in your relationship and you are certain that your date meets your other criteria. However, if children or getting married is important to you, don't leave it too long before tackling this conversation. I asked my now husband who already had two children if he wanted any more, within eight weeks of building trust and knowing him. Luckily, he said he loved children and wanted more with me!

Financial status

Knowing what someone does for a living may give away their financial status. It is also worth listening out for someone's financial commitments such as high mortgage payments, an expensive car, providing for children and/or ex wives/husbands or maintaining a luxurious lifestyle.

How to identify if you share any core values

The lifestyle choices that your date makes will provide clues as to what their core values are. Here are some examples:

- If your date invests a lot of time in their career, some of their core values could be money, status, achievement, success or fulfillment.
- If your date spends a lot of time with family and friends, some of their core values could be love, connection, support, fun and commitment.
- If your date is open, keeps to their word and treats other fairly, some of their core values could be honesty, integrity or respect.
- If your date loves having a good time partying or socializing, some of their core values could be fun, freedom or excitement.
- If your date enjoys spending time in nature, some of their core values could be peace, tranquility, calm and natural beauty.
- If your date loves travelling to new places, some of their core values could be adventure, stimulation or variety.

Be wary, though, that some people invest a lot of time in things that don't fulfill their core values. Someone could be a workaholic because they've got no one to go home to but would rather be fulfilling their values of love and connection with a life partner.

Here are some additional questions to get a better idea of someone's core values. These questions are fun and not too probing or offensive to ask in the early stages of dating:
- What's important to you in life?
- What would you do if you won the lottery?
- What would be your ideal job?
- If you didn't have to work, what would you do with your life?
- Where would you like to be in five years' time?
- Where would be your ideal location to live?

How to identify if you share a similar vision

Talking about the future with a date too early on can be scary and off-putting. Unless prompted by your date, steer clear of talking about future plans until you know that your date is a good match in terms of not having any cannot tolerates, having some ideals and a few can tolerates and shares some of your core values. When you are certain of all this, you have been dating for at least a couple of months and you have built trust up between you, you can start to ask specific questions about the future. For example, if your body clock is ticking and you're desperate to have children, make sure you find out whether your potential is interested in having children or not. If they don't even want to consider having children, you can walk away from the relationship at an early stage before you invest too much.

You now have a clearer idea of the kind of person that you want to share your life with. You are ready to take the next step to attract that special person.

Chapter 5

Building dating confidence

"Our deepest fear is not that we are inadequate. Our deepest fear is that we are powerful beyond measure. It is our light, not our darkness that most frightens us. We ask ourselves, Who am I to be brilliant, gorgeous, talented, fabulous? Actually, who are you not to be? You are a child of God. Your playing small does not serve the world. There is nothing enlightened about shrinking so that other people won't feel insecure around you. We are all meant to shine, as children do. We were born to make manifest the glory of God that is within us. It's not just in some of us; it's in everyone. And as we let our own light shine, we unconsciously give other people permission to do the same. As we are liberated from our own fear, our presence automatically liberates others."

From *A Return to Love,* by Marianne Williamson.

In **Chapter 1**, you learned how to overcome past relationship mistakes you were making and in **Chapter 2** you got clear about what you want in a long-term relationship. You are now getting closer to going out there and meeting your perfect match. To maximize your chances of meeting Mr or Mrs Right, you need to come across in the best possible way as the best possible you. Just as you build your confidence for a job interview and make sure you are dressed in the best way, so you must for a date.

By the time you have finished this chapter and applied the tools in it, you will be oozing confidence and sex appeal.

Is lack of confidence affecting your chances of meeting your perfect match?

Read the statements below and tick any that you agree with.

- I'm happy with my looks and comfortable in my skin.
- I like to take care of myself and look and feel good.
- People notice me when I'm out.
- I have good friends whom I can rely on.
- I stick up for myself and am generally not taken advantage of.
- I more often win arguments.
- I'm clear about what I have to offer to a potential partner.
- I consider myself a good catch.
- I'm not scared of talking to new people in new situations.
- I believe I can achieve anything I set my mind to.
- I receive compliments graciously.
- There's not much I would change about myself.
- I'm happy with my life so far.

Congratulations if you were able to tick one or more of the above statements, this shows that you are confident in one or more areas of your life.

If you were unable to tick ANY or ALL of the above statements then this chapter will help you to feel even more confident and increase your chances of meeting your perfect match.

Before I show you how to boost your confidence, I want to answer a question which I am often asked.

Won't I put potentials off by being overly confident?

My initial answer is that you can't be overly confident – you can be overly arrogant. Here is where I explain the difference between a confident and an arrogant person.

A confident person

- Is happy in their own skin and doesn't need to undermine others or boast to feel better about themselves.
- Is aware of their strengths and what they do well but comfortable enough in themselves to be humble and admit their weaknesses.
- In a position of authority will easily delegate to others and get them to carry out tasks which they are not so good at.
- Deals well with challenge or criticism from others and is not influenced by what others think of him/her.

An arrogant person

- Is not totally comfortable with who they are so needs to belittle and undermine others to feel good about themselves.
- Needs to show off overtly about their strengths and hides their weaknesses.
- In authority finds it hard to let go of control and entrust others.
- Doesn't like to be criticized and is sensitive to what other people think about him/her.

Barack Obama, Nelson Mandela, the late Anita Roddick (founder of Body Shop), Sting, Judi Dench and Kylie Minogue are all examples of confident people.

Simon Cowell, presenter and judge of American Idol in the US and the X Factor in the UK is an example of an arrogant person.

Obama, Mandela and Kylie Minogue's confidence inspires and creates a connection to others. I'll show you how you can develop your confidence to inspire and create a connection with potential perfect matches.

Confidence is the greatest aphrodisiac

- How much sex appeal would Madonna have if she lacked confidence?
- Would Mick Jagger have been a sex symbol without his onstage confident strutting?
- How attractive would the Sex and the City character Carrie Bradshaw be without her confident smile, easy-going attitude and her confidence to wear the most daring clothes?

One of the above is a sex symbol in her 50s and the other two are far from being conventionally good-looking.

When dating and looking for a new relationship you need to be confident about:

- Who you are
- Your physical appearance
- Your appeal to the opposite sex

How to feel confident about who you are

"It's not who you are that holds you back, it's who you think you're not."

— Author unknown

The main reason you lack confidence in who you are is because you have forgotten, are denying or are hiding who you are. The reasons for this can be having no time to express who you really are due to the time pressures of work and family or having years of your self-esteem being knocked by parents, partners, colleagues or bosses.

Here are some ways to remember to focus on who you are rather than what you are not:

1. **Make a list of your major achievements**
   Look over your life from childhood to the present time and write down all of your achievements, this can include:

   Passing exams, winning competitions, learning to play a musical instrument, voluntary work, making others feel special, travelling to foreign countries, getting a degree or other qualifications, succeeding in job interviews, making a difference at work, receiving promotion at work, having children, renovating a house, setting up a business, success in sport or other hobbies, overcoming illness, community work, planting and growing a garden, caring for a relative, moving to a different country, etc.

Your list of achievements will help you remember how much you have achieved and the strength, determination, passion and energy you used to accomplish them.

2. **Stop comparing yourself to others**
   One of the easiest ways to focus on who you are not, rather than who you are is to compare and think that friends, colleagues or even strangers are more attractive, more intelligent, more popular or just luckier than you are.

   The problem with comparing yourself in this way is that you are usually only focusing on one or two dimensions of the other person, so you are not taking into consideration that they have their failings, insecurities and weaknesses. They may just be better at hiding their failings and insecurities than you are.

3. **Practice an attitude of gratitude**
   You can counter comparing yourself to others by focusing on what you have to appreciate about yourself and your life. We all have something to be thankful for whether it be our health, family, friends, job, house, sense of humor, smile, ability to change, sunshine, walks in nature, children, pets, knowledge or strength.

4. **Don't confuse what you have with who you are**
   Owning a big house, flashy car or wearing designer outfits does not define who you are. It is ok if you enjoy material possessions and are not constantly striving for the next best thing. It is

not okay if you think that a bigger house, better car and more fashionable outfits are going to make you happy. Knowing and being comfortable with who you are will give you confidence and security.

Here is a powerful exercise to help you discover or remember who you really are.

Exercise 8 – What kind of person are you?

1. Email or write to three people whom you trust and who know you well (a friend, family member or colleague) to write back with their answers to one **or** all of the following questions:
   - What do you value about me as a friend, family member or colleague?
   - What do you consider are my best qualities?
   - Why do you think I would be a great catch for a future partner?

   If you think that doing this exercise sounds cringe-worthy, remember that those nearest and dearest to you will be happy to tell you how wonderful you are. You can also offer to return the favor and give your friend or family member or colleague feedback on what you value about them. You will have such a warm feeling after receiving the responses that it will make the exercise all worthwhile.
2. Enjoy the responses you receive; the people who wrote them are telling the truth and opening your eyes to how special you are.
3. Read over the responses and notice any common qualities or themes, for example, honesty, good listener, fun to be around, risk-taking, kindness, dependability.

4. Take three qualities which you think best describe you, for example, fun, loyal and thoughtful.
5. Repeat these three qualities to yourself at least once a day until they are embedded in your mind.
6. Remember and repeat aloud or in your head these three qualities whenever you are feeling doubtful, fearful, low or lacking in self confidence. You will believe in these qualities since three important people in your life agreed upon them.

Dawn's story

I met Dawn just after she had split up from her husband of 20 years. Dawn's self-esteem was at an all-time low and she could only think negatively about herself. She had no idea what she had to offer others and how much she meant to her family and friends. I asked Dawn to email three friends or family members to ask them what they valued about Dawn. Friends and family described Dawn as kind, generous, warm, determined, funny, wise, honest and elegant.

We selected three of the most important qualities: funny, wise and kind. I asked Dawn to repeat these at least once a day: "I am funny, wise and kind". I also asked Dawn to notice examples of when she behaved in a funny, wise or kind way.

After one week of repeating her three most important qualities and noticing when she displayed these qualities, Dawn's confidence grew and she started to realize that she played an important part in her friends' lives, became more confident in what she had to offer and started to receive compliments and recognition both inside and outside work. Repeating her three most important qualities really helped her in new and challenging situations.

How to feel confident about your appearance

"Sex appeal is fifty per cent what you've got and fifty per cent what people think you've got."

— Sophia Loren

With so much pressure from the media to look young and "perfect", it is no wonder that so many of us feel insecure about the way we look.

Mick Jagger, Sarah-Jessica Parker and Madonna prove that you don't need to be young or "perfect" looking to attract the opposite sex.

Tom Cruise may be short, dark and handsome, but he focuses on his physical assets, piercing blue eyes and well-toned body, rather than his imperfections.

Whenever you focus on how big your stomach is, how small you are, how unruly your hair is, how fat your thighs are, how bad your skin is, how big your nose is, how small your mouth is, how short your legs are, how wide your hips are, how big your bum is or any other physical imperfection which you **think** you have, you draw attention to it and encourage others to notice it too.

When you have been focusing on one or more physical imperfections for a long period of time, no matter how many people tell you that your bum is a normal size or your stomach looks flat or your nose adds character, you don't believe them. It would therefore be a tall order for me to ask you to change your perception of what you think makes you physically imperfect. Instead, I am going to help you to take the focus away from your perceived imperfections and on to your physical assets, just as Tom Cruise does.

We all have physical assets which make us attractive. One of my clients had beautiful hands with long slender fingers and perfectly shaped nails. Another client had a deep, sexy voice. Another client well-toned legs. Another a feminine, hour-glass figure. Another had broad, masculine shoulders. Because you have been focusing so much on your imperfections, you may not have even noticed your assets.

Exercise 9 – What are my physical assets?

1. Go through the list of physical features below and tick any which you think are your assets. If you feel okay about a physical feature listed, it is an asset to you.
2. If you can't identify any of the physical features below as an asset, get some feedback from trusted family and friends as to which ones they think are an asset to you (some physical features are more specific to men, some are more specific to women):

Physical Features

Long hair
Hair in good condition
Glossy hair
Striking hair color
Good haircut
Sassy short hair
Distinguished grey hair

Nice shaped face
Strong jaw line
Good bone structure
Open and warm face
Kind face
Sparkly eyes
Big eyes

How to Meet Your Perfect Match

Smiley eyes
Nice-colored eyes
Long eyelashes
Nicely shaped eyebrows
Striking eyebrows
Good skin
Youthful skin
Full lips
Sweetheart lips
Dainty mouth
Nicely shaped nose
Distinctive nose
Nicely shaped ears
Attractive voice
Deep voice
Feminine voice
Sexy accent
Broad shoulders
Strong muscular arms
Toned arms
Slender arms
Long fingers
Dainty wrists
Beautiful hands
Strong hands
Broad chest
Big bust
Perfectly formed bust
Small bust
Small waist
Defined waist
Hourglass figure
Cuddly figure
Defined abs
Flat stomach
Slim hips
Shapely hips
Round bottom (Beyoncé style)
Small, pert bottom
Muscular back
Toned back
Nice back
Long legs
Slender legs
Shapely legs
Muscular legs
Toned legs
Dainty feet
Attractive feet

3. Once you have identified at least three of your physical assets, create a plan as to how you can draw attention to them and encourage others to notice them. Here are some examples from my clients to give you some ideas:

Physical asset	How I can draw attention to it
Long, glossy hair	Wear my hair down instead of up and style it to look its best
Long slender fingers	Treat myself to a manicure or do my own, wear rings to draw attention to my fingers
Broad chest	Wear V-neck shirts to draw attention to my chest

Vanessa's story

Vanessa was a pretty blonde with blue eyes. She had always felt unconfident about her appearance and compared herself to her girlfriends, who always seemed to get more male attention than her. The reason that Vanessa didn't get as much male attention had nothing to do with her appearance but everything to do with her lack of confidence. She had learned how to fade into the background so men simply didn't notice her. When we went through Vanessa's physical features we identified three main assets: her blonde hair, pretty blue eyes and slender legs. We worked out how Vanessa could make the most of these assets and make them stand out. Firstly, Vanessa stopped wearing her hair up when going out, secondly she started wearing eye shadow and mascara to draw attention to her eyes and thirdly she started to wear skirts which showed off her slender legs. Over the following week, I asked Vanessa to notice if people reacted differently to her with her new look. The response was incredible, Vanessa noticed men paying her attentive and complimentary looks. Colleagues at work kept asking Vanessa if she had lost weight, had her hair cut or had a complete makeover. Friends commented that they didn't realize how pretty Vanessa was before. With this attention and compliments, Vanessa's confidence grew and she started to get noticed by eligible men.

Other tips to help you feel more confident about your appearance

- Go to http://www.trinnyandsusannah.com to learn how to take attention away from any of your "imperfections" including advice on thick ankles and calves, a flabby tummy and being flat-chested. There is also a good section on how to work out which colors best suit you.
- Get a new hairstyle or try a different hairdresser.
- Treat yourself to a color and style consultation with an image consultant. You can find one in your area by searching: www.colourmebeautiful.co.uk or try Caroline Shaw http://www.carolineshawcolours.com/
- Get a personal trainer who can support you in toning up or losing weight. Ask your local gym about which personal trainers are available.
- Have a free make-up consultation at a department store such as Debenhams, John Lewis or Selfridges in the UK.
- Book a free appointment with a personal shopper to update your wardrobe at John Lewis or Debenhams in the UK. Go to www.johnlewis.com or www.debenhams.com for more details.

How to feel confident about your appeal to the opposite sex

After completing exercises 8 and 9, you will be feeling better about who you are and how you look. However, after being on your own for so long or rejected so many times you may have lost some or all of your confidence in attracting the opposite sex. And, believe me, I too was in this situation before I came to understand the necessary balance of masculine and feminine energy in a relationship. I couldn't understand why men seemed to find me physically attractive but weren't interested in anything more than fun, why I quickly went off the "nice" guys who seemed to fancy me or why, when I did have longer relationships of a few months or so, that these men didn't want to commit further and couldn't explain why. Years later, after some honest feedback from wise friends and from reading some valuable relationships books, I realized that I had a predominant feminine energy system but had been acting in a masculine way in relationships which resulted in me either attracting feminine men (who I didn't fancy) or putting off more masculine men (who didn't fancy me), both resulting in failed relationships. My success in relationships began when I acknowledged, celebrated and communicated my feminine energy.

We all have and use a combination of masculine and feminine energy in our lives. Masculine energy is used by both men and women at work to achieve, reach targets and succeed. Feminine energy is used by both men and women when we relax, indulge in leisure and creative pursuits and relate to friends and family.

However, in a romantic relationship we will have a natural preference to express and exchange more of either our masculine or feminine energy with our partner.

To give you a better understanding of the necessary balance of feminine and masculine energy in a relationship, I will firstly share some theory.

The Swiss analyst Dr Carl Jung identified that men and women each have a feminine ("anima") and a masculine side ("animus"). Like the yin and yang in Chinese psychology and medicine, the feminine and masculine traits within us balance and complement each other. Your greatest appeal to a potential partner is your predominant feminine or masculine energy, which will complement their opposite predominant energy.

To feel fulfilled and whole, we all have a need to complement our either predominantly masculine or feminine energy. This explains why being with a partner with predominantly the opposite energy to ourselves gives us a sense of completeness and why when we are separated from them for long periods we feel incomplete. You can see examples of pairings of predominantly masculine and feminine energy in literature: Othello and Desdemona (Shakespeare), Elizabeth Bennet and Mr Darcy in Jane Austen's *Pride and Prejudice* and on screen, Clark Gable and Vivien Leigh in *Gone With The Wind*, Carrie Bradshaw and Mr Big in *Sex and the City* (she doesn't fall for Aidan in the same way, because he doesn't have enough masculine energy to complement her predominantly feminine energy).

These are obvious examples with the man having predominantly masculine energy and the woman having predominantly feminine energy. For a relationship to work **the man does not need to have the predominantly masculine energy** and **the woman the predominantly feminine energy**. There needs to be balance of masculine and feminine energy; this can also mean a man with predominantly feminine energy pairing with a woman with predominantly masculine energy. An extreme example of this is the former British prime minister Margaret Thatcher and her husband Dennis Thatcher.

American psychologist, Dr Pat Allen has used Jung's theories to develop a theory and strategy to help men and women balance their feminine and masculine sides and create fulfilling relationships. In her book, written with Sandra Harmon, *"Getting To I Do" The Secret to Doing Relationships Right!*, she writes:

"Successful relationships are an exchange of opposite energies, so the goal is to be able to make a clear decision about your energy system before you begin a relationship."

As well as displaying predominantly masculine or feminine energy in a relationship, Dr Pat Allen also identifies acting in a narcissistic way and describes it as:

*"Trying to use logic and feelings **equally**, which ultimately neutralizes both and ends intimacy through competitive conflict."*

Dr Pat Allen helps you to make a clear decision about your energy system by answering the question below:

Which is my greatest need – to be **cherished for my feelings** or **respected for my thoughts**?

If it is more important for you to be **cherished for your feelings** then your predominant energy system is **feminine**.

If it is more important for you to be **respected for your thoughts** then your predominant energy system is **masculine**.

To help you answer the question: Which is my greatest need – to be **cherished for my feelings** or **respected for my thoughts**? reflect on the situation below:

> You are having a discussion with your partner about arrangements for Christmas or another important holiday. There is a conflict between you as to whose family you spend Christmas or other holiday with.
>
> In this situation would it be more important for your **feelings** as to why you want to spend time with your family to be **cherished** by your partner (these could include feeling sad or disappointed that you haven't seen more of your family over the year or feeling anxious that your parents are getting older) or would it be more important for your **thoughts** as to why you want to spend time with your family to be **respected** by your partner (these could include facts about how much time you have spent with your family over the past year or the evidence that proves that your father hasn't got much time to live)?
>
> You could think or feel in this situation that you would want both your feelings to be cherished and your thoughts to be respected. However, you must choose whether having your thoughts respected or your feelings cherished would be **more important.**

Another way to assess whether your need to be **cherished for your feelings** or your need to be **respected for your thoughts** is more important is to count if you use "I feel…" or "I think…" more often when in discussions with family, friends or romantic partners. If you naturally use "I feel…" more often, then it is more important for you to have your feelings cherished and your predominant energy system is feminine. If you naturally use "I think…" more often, then it is more important for you to have your thoughts respected and your predominant energy system is masculine.

In her book, *Getting To I Do,* Dr Pat Allen also has a useful questionnaire on pages 64-70 to assess whether you want to be more masculine, feminine or narcissistic in a relationship.

Before the 1970s, men in the Western world were more often the sole breadwinners, protectors and didn't typically get involved in domestic tasks apart from DIY. Women were more often housewives who reared children and didn't work or worked in female professions such as teaching or nursing or in part-time, menial jobs. Male and female roles were much clearer during these times. The consequence was that men typically suppressed their feminine side, which meant that they found it harder to express their true feelings, and women suppressed their masculine side, which meant that it was harder for them to achieve anything outside of the home.

The feminist movement, beginning in the 1970s, made it more socially acceptable for women to have any type of career and pursue success and achievement outside of the home.

At the same time, men were allowed to show their more sensitive and feminine side. It has been liberating for women to realize their masculine side and men their feminine side. This liberation has, however, caused confusion and frustration for both men and women. Men can be unclear as to whether paying for dinner on a first date is courteous or offensive to an independent woman. Women can think that a man with all the traits of their best girlfriend would make them happy but at the same time are deeply attracted to more Alpha Male types. Women have become so skilled in using their masculine energy at work to achieve, succeed and progress that they find it hard to switch this off when they get home. The wonderful, typical, masculine traits that men can provide such as protection, reason and logic and good practical intelligence have been devalued by Western society so that some men have developed more feminine traits and become more best friends than romantic lovers to women. I'll reiterate that it will work for a man to display more predominantly feminine energy in a relationship and be more nurturing, sensual and sensitive if his female partner displays more predominantly masculine energy and is more protective, has more status and reason and logic.

What is masculine energy?

Masculine energy is expressed all around us and many of us use it to achieve in and outside work. It is goal-orientated, scheduled, directed, focused, self-disciplined, self-confident, strong and guiding.

Here are some behaviors and attitudes which show that you have a more predominantly masculine energy system in relationships *(please note that a man or a woman does not need to display **all** of these behaviors or attitudes to have a predominantly masculine energy system but will display more of these than the behaviors and attitudes listed under "What is feminine energy?")*:

- You feel comfortable making the first moves in the early stages of dating.
- You prefer to earn more money and provide more than your partner.

- You prefer to have more drive and ambition for work than your partner.
- It is really important for you to have your decisions respected.
- You need to have more control over big decisions in your relationship.
- You have a greater need and desire to protect your partner than nurture them.
- You use logic and reason to influence and win arguments.
- You are happy for your partner to take a bigger role in childcare/future childcare.
- You spend more time sorting out the practical things in your relationship, such as house and car maintenance.
- You have a need to keep your partner and family safe.
- You like to control the finances in your relationship.
- You prefer to initiate and dominate during lovemaking.
- You prefer to give in a relationship.

What is feminine energy?

Feminine energy is all around us and many of us crave it outside of work and find it in nature and creative pursuits such as music and dance. It is flowing, sensual, open, wild, unpredictable, caring, nurturing, life-giving and creative.

Here are some behaviors and attitudes which show that you have a more predominantly feminine energy system in relationships *(please note that a man or a woman does not need to display **all** of these behaviors or attitudes to have a predominantly feminine energy system but will display more of these than the behaviors and attitudes listed under "What is masculine energy?")*:

- You stand back and wait for the other person to make the first moves during the early stages of dating.
- You prefer your partner to earn more money and provide for you and your children/future children.
- You have less drive and ambition for your work than your partner.
- You need to have your feelings heard and acknowledged in a relationship.
- You prefer your partner to take the bigger decisions in your relationship.
- You have a greater need and desire to nurture your partner rather than protect them.
- You use emotion to influence and win arguments.
- You want to take a bigger role in childcare / future childcare than your partner.
- You spend more time maintaining relationships with friends and family than your partner.
- You feel a great need to make your partner and children happy.
- You prefer your partner to take control of the finances.
- You prefer your partner to initiate and be dominant during lovemaking.
- You prefer to receive in a relationship.

How can I tell If I am not acting from my preferred energy system in relationships and am attracting the wrong partners for me?

If you are not acting from your preferred energy system, for example, coming across as more masculine when your natural energy is feminine or coming across as feminine when your natural energy is masculine, you will be finding it hard to attract and maintain fulfilling relationships. Don't forget that as a woman your preferred energy system could be masculine and that as a man your preferred energy system could be feminine.

Here are some signs that you are not acknowledging and communicating your preferred energy system:

- You are a man or a woman and the people you fancy end up wanting to be friends not romantic partners.
- You are a woman who thinks that you should be going for the "nice guys" but you don't find them attractive.
- You are a man who likes the company of strong, independent women but relationships with them never work out
- You are a woman who attracts men who find you sexy but don't want to get involved in anything serious with you.
- You are a man who attracts women who enjoy your physical affection but are resistant or don't seem to enjoy having sex with you.
- You are a woman who attracts men who are intimidated and put off by your superior financial and career status.
- You are a man who attracts women who use and take advantage of your good nature.
- You are a woman who gives and gives in a relationship without getting much back.
- You are a man who attracts and takes advantage of women who fall at your feet and demand very little of you.

In Western society it is good that more emphasis is put on equality within relationships and that, for example, women are not compelled to do all the cooking and cleaning and that men can be more involved in childcare. However, to maintain the passionate and complementary dynamics of masculine and feminine energy within a relationship, it does not work to split **everything** equally. When couples try to do this, it causes stress for both parties since both people are having to behave outside of their preferred energy system and can also end up competing with each other. This is what Dr Pat Allen calls "narcissistic". See an example on the next page.

> ### Joan and Jeremy's story
>
> Joan's preferred energy system was feminine and Jeremy's was masculine. Joan had got so used to men and women having equal roles in her work as a teacher that she thought that this model should work for her and Jeremy. Joan and Jeremy both worked full-time so it worked well that they roughly shared household chores and cooking between them. Joan got tired of always organizing their social life and wanted Jeremy to pull his weight in this area. Any role within a relationship that has anything to do with relating to others such as keeping up with friends and family, remembering birthdays and organizing social events is typically a feminine type of activity (relatedness).
>
> Under duress but wanting to please Joan, Jeremy attempted to organize some of their social life. His attempts ended up frustrating more than pleasing Joan since he left any arrangements until the last minute and didn't do them in the way she wanted. Joan eventually gave up and started to appreciate the more masculine type of role which Jeremy played in navigating and driving him and Joan to social events.
>
> The moral of this story is not that a woman with preferred feminine energy needs to make all social arrangements or a man with preferred masculine energy needs to do all navigating and driving. The moral is to appreciate the other person's preferred energy, how they express it and what it brings to the relationship.

Like I was some of my clients are reluctant to embrace their preferred energy system and confuse feminine energy with weakness, losing control and submissiveness and masculine energy with dominance, force and control. Masculine and feminine energies are complementary rather than opposing, so each is strong and controlling in different ways. When a couple balance their masculine and feminine energies well, neither person has overall control in the relationship, each of them has more control in different areas of the relationship and each is happy about the areas each other has control over.

Here are some true stories to prove the value in acknowledging and communicating your preferred energy system.

> ### James' story
>
> James was an attractive guy in his late 30s with a good sense of humor and easy-going disposition. He had a good job and a nice home. His friends and family thought he was a great catch and couldn't understand why he was still single. He was caring and sensitive and believed in treating women with respect and as equals. He met lots of women through his work and in social situations. Some of these women seemed interested in him as a potential partner and then quickly lost any romantic interest but were keen to keep James as a friend. James had a mobile phone full of female friends' numbers. I helped James understand why he could attract female friends but not female lovers. We first identified whether it was more important for James' feelings to be cherished or his thoughts to be respected.
>
> James discovered that it was more important for his thoughts to be respected but he had thought that women found a sensitive, caring man more attractive than one who prioritizes logic and reason. I explained that a woman with predominantly masculine energy would find a more sensitive and caring man more attractive. The problem was that James was repelled by women with more career and money status than him or who wanted to take more control in the relationship than him. He needed to acknowledge and communicate more of his masculine energy in the first stages of dating. This didn't mean that he needed to come across as cold, uncaring and without feelings. We worked out a plan for James to communicate more of his masculine energy.

> **This included:**
>
> - James discussing his professional status instead of downplaying it (a woman with a predominantly feminine energy will be attracted to a man who has the ability to provide for her now or in the future).
> - James offering to pay for dinner on first dates instead of worrying about offending women by paying.
> - James talking as much as his dates in a conversation instead of letting them do all the talking. This gave him an opportunity to express his thoughts and logic.
> - James being protective towards his dates by offering to walk them to their car or to public transport and checking that they have got home safely.
> - James being proactive and taking control in the initial dating stages by phoning to arrange follow-on dates, choosing where to go on dates, appropriately making the first physical contact such as kissing or hugging.
> - James showing appreciation for his dates' feminine qualities such as their looks, choice of clothes and how they show sensitivity and care towards others.
>
> With these simple steps James found that dates stayed interested for longer rather than wanting to become friends. He also noticed that his dates responded to his masculine energy with charming feminine energy which he found a real turn-on.
>
> After several months of dating, James met a special girlfriend who looked, dressed and behaved in a feminine way and who appreciated James' status, the protection he could provide and logical thinking.

Catherine's story

Catherine was a confident, attractive woman who worked in a predominantly male environment. To get noticed in her work, she used her masculine energy to assert and prove herself. She wore lots of black suits to project a more serious, less fluffy image and restrained from showing any emotion at work or making any decisions based on emotion. Catherine was putting on quite an act to maintain this masculine façade and didn't realize how much stress she was putting herself under by maintaining it. She got so used to asserting her masculine energy at work that she found it difficult to step out of it in her personal life. Her friends thought of her as assertive and in some situations verging on aggressive. She wanted to have as much control and direction in her personal endeavors as she did at work. This drive served her well when she bought and renovated her first house. There was, however, one area of her life which she couldn't control and that was her romantic life. This was a source of great frustration for Catherine since she could put her mind to anything else she wanted in her life and get it. This formula did not work in attracting and maintaining relationships. She went out on the prowl like a tom cat in bars and clubs to attract men who she fancied. Men were at first seduced by her assertiveness and sexual energy but these encounters all began and ended in the same way. Catherine would take these men back to her house for a one-night stand and never hear from them again.

For a time, Catherine was proud of her conquests and had no desire for commitment, but after a while her self-esteem plummeted and she longed for more love in her life and for her feelings to be cherished. With my help, Catherine realized that she had been using her masculine energy in her relationships and denying her feminine side. Masculine energy had brought Catherine success at work so she subconsciously thought that asserting the same masculine energy in relationships would bring her similar success.

The problem was that Catherine was attracted to men with predominantly masculine energy who found her masculine energy exciting for a one-night stand but had no desire to enter into a relationship with someone who clashed and competed with them rather than complemented them. I made sure that Catherine did want to have the predominantly feminine energy in a relationship rather than predominantly masculine energy.

If it had turned out that Catherine, like at work, wanted to have the predominantly masculine energy in relationships, I would have advised her to attract a different type of man who was more sensitive, preferred not to make the first move and was happy for his partner to have more status and take more control in the relationship.

Catherine and I worked out a campaign for her to acknowledge and communicate more of her feminine energy in relationships. This included the following:

- Wearing more feminine clothes including skirts, flower patterns and pretty colors.
- Growing her hair longer and coloring it in a softer color.
- Smiling coyly at men who she found attractive, turning away and waiting for these men to approach her.
- Letting her male dates assert themselves by getting the waiter's attention, complaining about food being cold and ordering drinks.
- Listening to her dates' successes and achievements rather than jumping in with hers and trying to compete with them.
- Letting her dates open doors for her, help her to put on her coat, walk her to her car.
- Accepting compliments from her dates without playing them down or challenging them.

- Admiring and complementing her dates on their achievements, prized possessions (such as car and flat-screen TV) and logical thought.
- Making a special effort to look, smell and move in a sensual way for her dates.
- Letting her dates call her, set up dates and choose where to go on dates.
- Avoiding criticizing her dates' prized possessions, or something they have said or done.
- Letting her date make the first physical move such as kiss, hold hands or hug.
- Waiting for the man to decide when it was right to have sex for the first time.
- Waiting until she had got to know her partner before agreeing to have sex for the first time.
- Receiving attention, gifts, compliments, acts of service and time from her dates rather than over-giving herself.

At first Catherine thought that some of these behaviors made her weak and submissive and was resistant to trying them out, but gradually she became more and more comfortable with them since behaving in this way resulted in her attracting men who truly wanted to love and cherish her.

She ended up marrying a man with predominant masculine energy and they continue to complement each other and the passion has stayed alive in their relationship.

> ### Caroline's story
>
> Caroline had a high-flying successful career and exemplified being an independent woman. She managed to attract equally successful men with career and material status. Her relationships fizzled out after a six-month honeymoon period when she started to clash and compete with her partners. She wanted to show how she was more successful than them and resented them achieving more than her. She wanted them to respect her opinions and decisions and ended up in heated arguments when they challenged her opinions and decisions. The men she dated lost interest and emasculated for not being respected more for their opinions and achievements. I helped Caroline to realize that her preferred energy system was masculine and that she had been attracting men with a preferred masculine energy system. Her relationships failed since there wasn't enough complementary feminine energy to keep them alive. I encouraged Caroline to try attracting and dating men with a preferred feminine energy. To do this she needed to attract men who were initially shyer than her and wanted a woman to approach them. These men who preferred to be seduced tended to earn less money than Caroline and be more sensitive and nurturing. In turn, they respected Caroline's drive, ambition and her opinions. Caroline ended up marrying and having a baby with David. They have continued to be very happy as Caroline has returned to work and David works part-time and looks after their child. Caroline is fulfilled as a working mother and David is happy working fewer hours and having more time to spend with his daughter and do voluntary work.

You have now learned how to develop and communicate your confidence and discovered more about the necessary balance of masculine and feminine energy and how going against your preferred energy in a relationship will lead to dissatisfaction and failure. If you are still lacking in confidence or unsure as to which is your preferred energy or are resistant to communicating either your feminine or masculine energy in a relationship, read Dr Pat Allen's book for a more in-depth explanation or get in touch with me about relationship coaching.

Recommended reading

"Getting To I Do" The Secret to Doing Relationships Right!

— Dr Patricia Allen and Sandra Harmon

This book provides an excellent explanation of how to balance masculine and feminine energy in a relationship and how to navigate yourself through the different stages of a relationship. It is written for women but relevant and useful for men as well.

http://www.drpatallen.com Dr Patricia Allen's website with details of her books, DVDs and classes. This also includes an excellent book list.

CHAPTER 6

Dating success

You have now worked through what was holding you back, know what you want, are oozing confidence and sex appeal and are almost ready to hit the town and the internet. Before you do, you need to make sure that you are coming across in the best possible way and that you are attracting rather than repelling the opposite sex.

Male and female participants at my **How to Meet Your Perfect Match Workshops** are often worried that they are either not picking up signals from potentials or are not giving off the right signals to potentials. When we say the word "signal", we actually mean body language since 55% of our message is communicated through what our bodies are doing, 38% through the tone of our voice and only 7% through the actual words we speak. This is especially important in flirting and dating situations since we usually decide whether we fancy someone new or not before they have even had a chance to open their mouths. Also, don't forget that a first impression is made within two to three seconds and the thing about first impressions is that we only get one chance to make them.

We all subconsciously give off messages as to how we are thinking and feeling through our facial expressions, hand gestures and the way we stand, sit and move.

In dating situations most of us feel vulnerable and are not going to approach someone who we think will reject us.

I remember being out with some male friends during my single days and them noticing that I was pretty good at attracting male attention in bars and clubs. I asked them why they thought I could easily get male attention. Their answer was, "Candy, you make it easy for guys to approach you since you are smiley, open and don't come across as scary and intimidating." My male friends had observed too many girls in bars and pubs who came across as standoffish, miserable and way too cool. I have to admit that I was good at attracting male attention, but often it would be the wrong kind!

You may be unable to even contemplate going on a date since you are scared stiff of either being rejected or having to reject the other person. You may be wondering why you are often asked out on first dates but not on second or third dates.

This chapter will help you to understand what you might have been doing wrong in your approach or response to the opposite sex, how to handle rejection effortlessly and reject others graciously, how to come across as your best possible self during first dates and how to make sure you get invited on second and third dates.

How to attract and approach the opposite sex

The advice given below is about how to communicate your predominant masculine or predominant feminine energy clearly to the opposite sex through your body language.

Do you remember me saying in Chapter 5 that confidence is the greatest aphrodisiac? We just can't resist that man or woman who is totally at ease with who they are and the body they are in, no matter what they look like.

The great and annoying thing about body language is that it directly communicates how we are feeling. This can be annoying when we want to hide our feelings and our facial expressions give us away. We can, however use it to our advantage.

> **Try this experiment**: bring your head down so that your chin almost touches your chest, look down towards the floor and hunch your back so that you are even closer to the ground. How does this make you feel? This is the typical body language of someone who is depressed and down. Now try this one, sit tall with your shoulders back and your chest open, look forward and smile. This is the typical body language of someone who is confident and at ease. It is hard to feel happy when you are faced towards the ground. It is hard to feel down when you are sitting tall and smiling.

I'm going to show you how to use body language in dating situations to help you exude that potent aphrodisiac – confidence. Don't worry if at first it feels a bit false; the expression "fake it till you make it" really does work with body language and practice makes perfect.

How to communicate confidence through body language

Hold your head high

A raised head is the sign of someone who is confident and takes control. The more confident we feel about ourselves, the higher we will hold ourselves. It doesn't matter how tall you are, that magical thing called presence expresses our confidence. Tom Cruise, Robert De Niro and Reese Witherspoon don't let their actual height hold them back.

Deep breaths

When you are nervous or anxious you start to breathe more shallowly and restrict the amount of oxygen flowing to your brain. This has a detrimental effect on your thinking and can lead to you speaking too quickly and putting your foot in it. The moment you start to slow down and breathe deeper, you start to feel calmer and come across as less anxious and more in control.

Stand tall

Stand with your feet firmly planted on the floor so that you feel as stable as possible. Pull your shoulders back and down so that your chest is open, this allows you to breathe more deeply, hold your head high and face directly towards the person you are interacting with.

Make eye contact

You have probably been in a situation with someone who couldn't meet your eye and it made you feel pretty uncomfortable. Confident people are not afraid of connecting with others and the simplest way to do this is to make and maintain appropriate eye contact. I say "appropriate" since if you completely stare someone out, the other person will think you are some kind of weirdo and avoid you at all cost. If you observe two people who are at ease and comfortable with each other, they will take turns making eye contact, looking away and making eye contact again. Also, remember that to maintain a connection with someone, you don't need to constantly look directly into their eyes, you can focus on different areas of their face and even focus on the bridge of their nose instead of their eyes.

Focus on your assets

We all have bits of our bodies that we don't like, put these to the back of your mind and focus on your greatest assets, whether it be your smile, voice, legs, boobs, hands, hair or butt.

Go back to when you did feel confident

When confidence wanes repeat in your head compliments people have given you in the past. This will automatically signal your body language to change since you will be feeling differently. Notice how you feel and how your body language changes when you think of a happy event and now try the same and think of a sad event from your life.

Exercise 10

> Before going speed dating, approaching strangers in bars or going on any actual dates, it is worth practicing your new confidence-building skills in non-date situations. You can practice holding your head up high and walking tall down the street and at work: notice how people react to your new, confident stance. You can practice making eye contact and smiling at strangers in any situation: on the metro, on a walk, out shopping, at work or at other car drivers in a traffic jam. You've got nothing to lose practicing with strangers since you are unlikely to see them again!

Clients often ask me:

"How do I pick up on signals that someone likes me? I'm sure I'm missing out on some and letting potential dates slip away."

The first thing I say in response to this question is that you have to believe that people of the opposite sex are giving off positive signals to you. If you believe that no one will find you attractive, your belief becomes a self-fulfilling prophecy. Reread **Chapter 3, Your Perfect Match – what's holding you back from meeting The One,** if you don't believe that anyone would be attracted to you.

If you believe that there are people out there giving you positive signals but you don't know what they are or are missing them, read on for some of the most obvious ones.

Seven signs that HE is interested

- **His eyebrows** will rise and fall very subtly; this makes his eyes wider and brighter so they literally draw you in. They will also stay raised as you're talking and he shows he's into you.
- **Read his lips**: if he's into you, his lips will part for a moment.
- His **nostrils** flare and his face generally opens, making him look friendly and approachable.
- He'll try to attract your attention, which could be any **exaggerated movement** such as adjusting his tie.
- He'll stand **directly** in front of you to show full attention and lean forwards to get closer.
- He'll let you see him **checking out your body** – not much subtlety here!
- He'll sit with legs spread to show you his **crotch** – again, he's not leaving much to the imagination!

Eight signs that SHE is interested

- She smiles at you, whether a half or full smile.
- She looks at your **mouth** most of the time, subconsciously thinking what it would be like to kiss you.
- She quite unsubtly eyes your **derrière** up and down.
- She shrugs her **shoulders** very quickly, showing excitement.

- She'll let a strap or a sleeve full off her **shoulder** revealing this erotic area.
- She touches her **neck**, drawing attention to another erotic area.
- She'll do a Liz Hurley and stand with her **legs slightly apart,** weight on one foot and **hips** tilted.
- She can't stop looking at you and sends short, repetitive **glances** your way.

What to do when you feel confident and have the other person's attention

Here are some ways to make sure you keep the opposite sex interested.

The three-step" I'm interested" look for women

Whatever you do, if someone looks your way for an extended period of time (more than four seconds) don't forget to show that you are interested. Here is a sure-fire way to get your message across that the world's best flirts naturally use.

- Make eye contact back with the person for longer than you would usually feel comfortable doing.
- Look down and to the side.
- Look back up again to get eye contact with a half smile.

Be yourself

We are most attracted to people who come across as **genuine** and comfortable in their skin, not by people who are out to impress.

Intelligence pulls

Look intelligent by using direct eye contact, giving your

full attention to the other person and talking about things you know something about.

Forget cool and aloof

Look **friendly** and **approachable**, smiling is contagious and will warm someone to you.

Mirroring or copying someone else's body language makes them like you. If you're sitting, standing or leaning in a similar way to another person, you are sub-consciously tuning into what that other person is feeling, which builds instant rapport. We naturally mirror each other's body language when we like someone. Try observing a happy couple next time you are out in a restaurant or bar and notice the dance of their body language as one person mirrors the other person's facial and hand gestures and the other person follows. You'll know a couple is in trouble when they are out of synch and not mirroring each others' body language!

How to handle and deal out rejection

I work with many clients who won't even try online dating, speed dating, respond to advances in bars and at singles parties or go on blind dates because they are wracked with the fear of either being rejected or having to reject the other person. Believe me, I know all about fear of rejection. In my 30s, I made a conscious decision to stop dating and even getting interest from men since I was so tired of hearing lines like "it's not you, it's me" and waiting for men to call after a first date who clearly had no intention of ever calling. I also got fed up with handing out rejection to men who wouldn't take no for an answer. I then realized that if I wasn't willing to be rejected or do some rejecting myself, I wouldn't fulfill my dream of meeting my soul mate. I want to make it easier for you to deal with rejection with my advice below.

David Rock, a neuro-leadership consultant, says: "When you feel rejected socially, the same circuits in your brain light up as when you feel physical pain." No wonder we struggle so much with rejection.

We commonly face rejection when we ask for a promotion, send off CVs or go for job interviews. Job searching can be a very testing time, but most of us accept that we need to go through some kind of rejection to get the right job.

We don't hesitate to send off another CV or go to another interview if at first we don't succeed.

It is far harder to bounce back and go on another date than it is to book that next interview. I have coached accomplished sales people who live and breathe rejection in their work, but find it impossible to handle rejection in a dating situation. We tend to invest more of ourselves emotionally into any dating situation, so we take this type of rejection more personally and feel it more intensely.

Here comes the hard news – if you want to meet the right person, you are going to have to do some rejecting and expect to be rejected yourself. Otherwise, you could end up settling for "Mr or Mrs Not So Right".

How to reject others

The best way to learn how to reject others is to think about how you prefer to receive rejection. You may be tired of hearing clichés such as "let's just be friends." You may resent people who have said they would phone after a first date and never did.

If you would like to be rejected in a more honest and integral way, then make sure that you reject others in this way. It is always worth beginning by saying what you have enjoyed about the date or the time you have spent together, for example, "I really enjoyed hearing about your travel experiences." The next step is to be honest without being cruel.

Generally, we find it hardest to reject dates when we are not physically attracted to them. A good way to handle this is to say, "I don't want to meet again because I don't feel that there is enough chemistry between us."

Remember that lack of chemistry is not just because someone looks a certain way; it is literally the combination of your two energies, which causes a sexual attraction. This means that you could feel a lack of chemistry with someone who, on the surface, you think is a real looker!

Dealing with being rejected

Here are my top tips on how to deal with rejection:

1. Every "no" that you receive is bringing you closer to the right "yes" and your perfect match.
2. Think of a time when you rejected a potential date or relationship – what was going through your mind? This will help you to understand why someone may be rejecting you.
3. Take stock and put things into perspective: avoid using "always" or "never," for example, "men/women **always** reject me" or "I'll **never** meet anyone."
4. Remember that each date or relationship (however, short) is teaching you something and will lead you closer to the right person.
5. Ensure that you analyze the situation accurately and quickly and avoid phoning everyone you know to moan and prolong your suffering.
6. Avoid "binge" eating, drinking, moaning and shopping to get over the rejection. Bingeing brings short-term relief and then makes you feel worse.
7. Instead of bingeing, indulge yourself in what I call a "self-esteem ritual" such as, connecting

with people who value you highly, doing something which you have put off for months, doing something you are afraid of or doing something which makes you look and feel fabulous. I had one client who would book something nice to do the day after every date she went on, such as lunch with friends. If the date went well, she could celebrate with friends, if the date didn't go so well she would have company to commiserate with her.

8. Get back on your bike and on the dating scene!

Handling rejection is not easy, but the more we practice, the easier it gets and we can have a lot of fun along the way!

How to make the most of first dates

A first date is like a job interview, you really want to make the best impression you can and be invited back. Like a job interview, there is so much to prepare for and think about:

- What do I say on a first date and how do I make sure that I don't dry up?
- What do I wear?
- Where to go on a first date?
- What do I do at the end of the date?
- Do I kiss on the first date?

Read on for the answers to these questions.

What to say on a first date

A common fear for people new to the dating scene is, "What if I dry up and don't have anything to say on my first date?" It is worthwhile preparing ahead of the date to keep the conversation flowing. Firstly, think about conversation icebreakers. Don't be afraid of starting off with the obvious such as:

> "How was your journey here?"
>
> "How has your day been?"

Move on to more interesting conversation and if you have met or spoken to the person before, pick up a previous topic. Follow the golden conversational rule of using open questions beginning with how, what, when and why. Avoid closed questions, which elicit nos and yesses, these usually start with "do", and "is/are"

People usually love to talk about themselves so ask questions that allow them to do this, such as:

> "What do you enjoy doing outside of work?"
>
> "What's most important to you in your life?"
>
> "Where do you like to go on holiday?"

In a dating conversation, men will tend to speak more than women. This is because women are generally better listeners.

As a woman on a first date, make sure that you get your points across and don't be afraid of interrupting to do so. Guys – make sure you take a breather and allow your date to speak.

As important as what to say on a first date is what **not** to say. Avoid mention of exes and if the other person asks keep your answer brief. There is plenty of time for this subject if you continue seeing each other. Also, keep conversation relatively light and avoid politics and religion. Avoid talking for too long about your children, pets or work – this could give the impression that you don't have space for a significant other in your life.

If you are grappling with shyness and find it difficult to talk to anyone new, Leil Lowndes' book, *How to Talk to Anyone*, is packed with tips, advice and techniques to try.

What to wear on a first date

Men are very visual so impressed by what women wear on dates. Women are generally more observant and critical about how others dress. This means that it is important for both sexes to carefully consider their choice of outfits.

Like conversation, plan in advance. Women are generally impressed by men who have taken some effort over their appearance. Pay attention to the basics such as shaving, ironing your shirt and smelling nice without drowning yourself in aftershave.

Don't wear the clothes you feel most comfortable in, if this means an old pair of trousers and t-shirt.

Make an effort and wear something smart and match trousers, shirts and shoes. Women have a keen eye for shoes so make sure yours are polished!

For women, the same rules apply in terms of making an effort for your date. However, understatement can be far more appealing than overplaying it with a killer sexy outfit. Plunging necklines have become commonplace but you may want your date to make eye contact rather than have their eyes glued to your cleavage all night.

General rules for a first date include looking smart and presentable but keeping your more daring and sexy outfits to potential later dates when you have got to know each other better.

Where to go on a first date

Where to go can depend on how well you have got to know your first date. If you are going on a relatively blind date, it is best to arrange a shorter date such as lunch or coffee. It is always good to have something planned after the date so that you have an excuse to leave, just in case conversation isn't flowing.

If you have already met your date at a party or through friends and you know there is chemistry, then it could be better to plan a longer date. Going for dinner is the top choice for most first dates since it allows for lots of conversation.

Be careful to choose somewhere quiet enough to hear each other but with enough of an atmosphere so that you're not completely on your own.

An activity-based first date can also be a good way of finding out more about each other and provides focus, if conversation dries up. One of my most imaginative first dates was when an ex-boyfriend invited me to go sailing – quite apt for a sailing instructor and very fun for me!

Don't plan too adventurous or quirky first dates unless you already know the person fairly well. Like adventurous outfits, they are best kept for when you've got to know each other better.

What do you do at the end of a date?

The evening is coming to a close; you're thinking about getting your last train home, you've really enjoyed your time together. Or, you could be secretly clock checking, thinking of all the things you would rather be doing and working out how long you need to stay so as not to look rude before making your excuses to go. What do you do next? The way you end a date can affect your chances of ever seeing your date again.

If your date hasn't tried to rush away after a couple of hours, you have noticed some encouraging body language, especially any mirroring or leaning towards you, then you need to clearly communicate that you would like to meet again. If you are a man or a woman with predominant masculine energy, you need to take the lead at the end of the date.

You need to avoid any **hesitation** or **tentativeness** such as "Maybe, if you would like, we could possibly see each other again?" or "Let me know if you would like to meet again". Instead, communicate your confidence and ability to take control with something like "I had a great evening, I'll call you to arrange to meet again." If you say you are going to call, make damn sure you do. If you are the man or the woman with predominant feminine energy, make sure that you show your interest when the other person takes control. Don't leave any doubt in the other person's mind that you are interested. You can respond with something like "I had a great evening too and look forward to hearing from you."

If your date has tried to rush away, has shown signs of being bored, has turned away from you and is not mirroring your body language, they are probably not that interested. If you are interested, you can use the line "I really enjoyed the evening/your company, and you have my number/email to get in touch if you are interested in meeting again." This leaves it open for the other person to get in touch if you misread the signals and they are interested. It also makes it easier for the other person not to outrightly reject you.

Whether the date has gone well or not so well, it is polite and gracious as a man to make sure that the woman gets home safely. This could mean walking her to her car or to a train station or bus stop.

Do you kiss on a first date?

Obviously, if you have already kissed when you met at a party or club or bar then it makes sense to continue with the tradition. If you are meeting the date for the first time, apply caution. A friendly kiss on the cheek shows respect and warmth. Tread very carefully when kissing a first date on the lips. You really need to be sure that this intimate gesture will be appreciated, otherwise it could seriously backfire. Your setting for the kiss also plays a part. We feel more comfortable kissing on a first date in darker surroundings where there is less risk of being spotted. The best things in life are often worth waiting for and so much better when we get them – just like a first kiss after a couple of dates!

How to behave in the initial dating stages

You may have had the experience of being asked out on dates but these first dates have never materialized into second or third dates. Or you may have gone on two to four dates and then the other person has lost interest.

Your lack of success in being invited to go on second, third or fourth dates could be down to attracting the wrong types of men/women **(see Chapter 1)**, not being clear about what you want **(see Chapter 4)**, or simply lack of compatibility or chemistry. In some cases, it is none of the above and is more to do with the way you come across during those initial, crucial dating phases.

There are five crucial dating stages which you need to be aware of:

1. **Infatuation**

    This is the initial phase where you get a chance to show that you are attracted to and get to know your potential partner. You can be infatuated on a physical, emotional, mental and spiritual level.

2. **Testing**

    This is the second crucial stage, when we are working out whether this is the right person for us or not. Without understanding this stage we can falsely think that because we have feelings of uncertainty that this is not the right person for us. I work with lots of clients who are ready to give up at this stage; with my help many of them continue with the relationship and end up being very happy. At this stage, it is easy for men and women to drift away and move onto the next conquest. It is a time when we can dismiss potential partners for petty and ridiculous reasons such as the shape of their legs or the socks they wear. There is a danger at this stage of not getting to know the other person better and allowing the relationship to grow.

3. **Initial commitment**
   This is the third stage, where you want to enter into a monogamous relationship and stop dating anyone else. This is the time to drop your guard a bit, relax and spend more time with your partner. You have to be careful at this stage not to get too complacent; don't stop making an effort to make your partner feel special, which can include dressing to impress our partners, romantic gestures and arranging special dates.

4. **Comfort**
   This is the stage where we experience true intimacy and we can be more relaxed and let our partners see our best as well as our worst side. This includes emotional as well as physical intimacy.

5. **Lifelong commitment**
   This is when you feel certain that you are with the person you want to marry or make a lifelong

commitment to. The four previous stages prepare you for this final stage. Before getting married or making a lifelong commitment, you gather positive experiences to help you through the tough times and learn how to resolve conflict within your relationships.

Since this chapter is all about dating, I'm going to focus on the initial infatuation stage.

Surviving the infatuation stage

This is the stage where we show our dates our most positive self so that they can feel most attracted to us. There are some important things to remember at this stage.

Women or men with a predominant feminine energy need to promote themselves

At this stage a man or a woman with predominantly masculine energy can think that talking endlessly about themselves will impress the woman or man they are with. They especially think this when the woman/man keeps asking them questions. Meanwhile, the woman/man is thinking "why doesn't he ask me anything?" Women/men at this stage need to interrupt politely with something like "I'd just like to add.." or "I think…"

Both sexes need to hold back physically

Both sexes can want to cut to the chase and get physical due to overwhelming physical attraction or a desire to get intimate. Women need to remember that the release of oxytocin during sex can bond you to a partner and make you feel great intimacy but the man will not necessarily feel the same way. Men need to resist the temptation to get physical and spend time getting to know the woman first. It'll be worth the wait. Waiting gives the relationship more of a chance to develop. I have an expression which I use with any of my clients who rush into relationships physically; "quick in, quick out".

Men and women with a predominant feminine energy need to hold back emotionally

Just as some of you can rush into physical intimacy, some of you can rush into emotional intimacy because you feel comfortable and a strong physical attraction. But, at this stage, you don't know the other person well enough to be emotionally intimate. Just as someone coming on too strong physically can turn you off so can someone coming on too strong emotionally. This means holding back from saying "I like you" or "I love you". It also means holding back from asking for too much emotional support at this stage. This can wait until later – you don't want to come across as too needy. This is a time to communicate your mysterious side, leaving the other person dying to find out more about you.

Men like to make women happy and don't expect things in return

Men gain great pleasure from doing things to make their women happy. This can include all those lovely true gent gestures like helping a woman put on her coat, opening the car door for her and letting ladies go first. It can also include bigger gestures such as booking a classy restaurant or paying for a nice meal. My female clients often don't believe me on this one because they have been attracting the wrong types of men who are not in it for the long term.

Women make the mistake of treating a man the way they would like to be treated

This means that women respond to a man's attentiveness by playing tit for tat and insisting that she return his gestures.

This could include insisting on paying for the meal next time or even fussing over a man and helping him put on his coat. Instead, the man wants appreciation and to know you have made him happy. It is much better to enjoy a man's attention and express gratitude with a simple thank you and a smile.

Women need to express their needs

This is true at any stage of a relationship but the sooner you start expressing your needs, the better. Women tend to be disappointed by men who don't automatically read their minds and anticipate their needs. What men are great at is giving a woman what they want when they know what it is that a woman wants! There is nothing demanding or wrong with expressing needs. In fact, having your needs met prevents conflict. The types of needs that women need to express early on can include the type of restaurant they like to go to and when it is convenient to call. This sets a good foundation to express what you might deem as more demanding needs later on in the relationship.

The aim of this chapter was to boost your confidence by helping you feel more prepared for going on first and subsequent dates. You are now prepared to get out there and try different places and methods to meet your perfect match in the next chapter.

CHAPTER 7

Where and how to meet your perfect match

I know that a lot of you will rush straight to this chapter and bypass the first four. The truth is that you could try hundreds of different places, methods and activities to meet someone but if you haven't:

- Broken free from destructive relationship patterns
- Built your self-esteem
- Overcome your negative beliefs
- Got clear about the type of person and relationship that you deserve
- Built confidence in what you have to offer in a relationship
- Learnt how to handle the ups and downs of dating

…you are unlikely to be open to a different "type" and you will end up attracting the same losers, users and players that you have always attracted. Worse still, your attitude and negative belief will stop you from attracting anyone. If you feel like you have explored every potential dating avenue from widening your circle of friends to evening classes to internet dating to speed dating to singles nights and you are still not meeting Mr or Mrs Right, you need to reread **Chapters 1-4** or contact me for some one-to-one coaching for help on identifying the obstacles holding you back.

If you have fully digested and taken on board advice

and guidance from **Chapters 1-6**, well done. Read on for the best ways to meet your perfect match.

> ### MEGAN'S STORY
>
> Megan came to one of my workshops and then continued to have coaching with me. When I first met 40-something Megan, I was struck by her youthfulness and elegant dress style. On top of this, Megan was a highly intelligent and well-trained doctor with very good social skills and a wide circle of friends and interests. Megan sought my guidance to help her improve the relationship area of her life, which had been lacking for many years. She had a history of failed and destructive relationships and was extremely skeptical as to how I could help her. In our coaching we identified why Megan had repeated destructive relationship patterns and helped her let go of the past. We continued with smashing Megan's negative beliefs. Just as we were ready to start writing Megan's online profile and signing her up for internet dating, a new neighbor moved in next door to her. This neighbor was a tall, single man in his 50s but not at all Megan's type. Within a few weeks, the male neighbor got to know Megan and started to show his affection with caring and protective acts of service, including driving her to work when her car broke down, keeping an eye on the house while Megan went away and fixing her dripping tap.
>
> After a while, he made his feelings clear to Megan and how attractive he found her but remained an absolute gentleman. Megan was lapping up the attention, felt her self-esteem soaring and started to truly enjoy her neighbor's company, still insisting that he wasn't her type. With some encouragement from myself and friends, she came to realize that her male neighbor was everything that she had asked for in a man and could make her very happy and she embarked on a committed relationship with him. Megan admits that she wouldn't have given her neighbor a second look if she hadn't smashed her destructive relationship patterns and negative beliefs.

How to create a dating strategy

Just as experienced investors take a portfolio approach by selecting a collection of investment assets that has collectively lower risk than any individual asset, I recommend creating a **portfolio strategy for dating.** In your quest for love, you may not be at risk of losing your life savings, but you do risk losing faith, patience and heart from repeated rejections and disappointments. As one of my now-married male friends has always said, "dating is a numbers game". You need to make sure that you are opening yourself up to as many opportunities as possible to meet as many potential perfect matches as possible. If you are only focusing your efforts on one or two methods such as meeting the opposite sex through friends and social networks, you will come across as more desperate during these situations since they are your only option. We all know the smell of desperation and how it immediately turns us off. The other advantage to creating a portfolio strategy for dating is that you truly can't predict where you will meet your perfect match so best to keep your options open!

There is one method that I recommend all my clients include in their dating portfolio – internet dating. Many of my clients recoil and cringe when I advise this since they say they want to meet someone "naturally" or don't have the time to devote to online dating or they've met nothing but pen pals and losers online. Later, I'll explain how you can overcome these fears.

Where to meet the opposite sex

Dance classes

Ceroc, salsa and tango dance classes are all good places to meet men and women. Tango typically attracts more men than salsa and ceroc but is more difficult to learn. Salsa and ceroc classes are fun and informal and are a great opportunity to meet others and build your social circle, even if you don't meet the one on the dance floor. Dance classes are also a great way to build up confidence with the opposite sex, if you have been out of the dating scene for a while. You have to get pretty up close and personal in some of those dance moves!

For more information in the UK try:
> http://www.uksalsa.com/
> http://www.ceroc.uk.com/
> http://www.danceweb.co.uk/tango/

In the US or Europe or other places around the world, try "local dance classes" as a search term in your preferred search engine.

If you've ever had a bad experience at dance classes with lecherous men trying it on, seek out a different class. You should never tolerate this behavior in a dance class.

Speed dating

Remember that more women are interested in signing up for speed dating since they prefer to network and meet potential dates face to face. Speed dating is a great place to practice your flirting and dating skills if you're feeling a bit rusty or want to develop some of the skills you learnt in Chapter 6. You will meet an average of 10-20 dates in an evening and you can select a speed dating event local to your home or work. More on speed dating in the **How to get the most out of speed dating** section.

Singles nights

At singles nights and parties you can choose from a bigger selection of people and have a longer period of time to get know potential dates. Singles nights usually include ice-breakers to encourage you to speak to as many participants as possible, speed dating and activities such as mini dance classes.

Singles events

Some of my clients have reported that they prefer singles events where people come together around a focused activity such as wine tasting, a dinner, walk, cycle ride or theatre trip. There are also singles salsa nights. One of my clients highly recommends singles wine tasting and says, "I felt more relaxed at singles wine tasting evenings since they felt less contrived than speed dating and did actually result in dates".

For more information in the UK try:
> http://www.single-london.com/events.htm
> http://www.uksinglesnight.co.uk/
> http://www.grapevinesocial.com/

In the US or Europe or other places around the world, try "singles nights/events + your town or city" as a search term in your preferred search engine.

Introduction agencies

Take the legwork out of meeting that special someone and use their skills and experience to match you with someone from their database. More on introduction agencies in the **How to get the most out of introduction agencies** section.

Personal ads

These are small ads in newspapers where you can read a small synopsis about someone and then dial a number to hear more about that person from a recorded message. I advise that online dating, where you usually get to see a photograph and read more information, is a more efficient and cheaper option than personal ads.

Social networks

I am referring to social networks where you meet in person rather than network online. These are a great place to meet other like-minded people and widen your social circles so you may not necessarily meet your perfect match but could meet some contacts who could introduce you to that special someone.

www.meetup.com is a great resource for anyone around the world (you can do a search by country and town) who is wishing to join like-minded people to learn or share an interest. Groups range from walking to Spanish language to dachshund dogs to beer lovers to aspiring entrepreneurs to mountaineering to NLP to EFT to dance to photography to meditation.

http://www.ivc.org.uk/ is a national UK network of social events and clubs aimed at professionals, graduates and like-minded people. They have nearly 50 clubs and around 5,000 members across the UK.

http://www.spiceuk.com has social groups around the UK and offers adventure activities, personal development workshops and social events for both single people and those in relationships.

http://citysocialising.com is a UK club for sociable, laid-back professionals through which you can connect with new local friends with shared interests in the real world.

http://www.toastmasters.org/ if you're interested in improving your public speaking skills and gaining confidence, Toastmasters weekly events are an excellent way to meet new people. You can search for a group by country and city.

If you are based outside the UK, you can do an online search using the term "social networks + your city, area or country" in your preferred search engine.

Singles holidays and breaks

These are a great way to get to know other singles over a longer period of time. They are also a great option if all of your friends are paired off and you have no one to go on holiday with. Going on a singles short break can be a good way to test if a group holiday is your cup of tea. Some well-established companies in the UK and the US include:

www.explore.co.uk
http://www.singlesholidays.com
http://www.trekamerica.com/

The gym

Your local gym is a great place to meet and socialize with others. If you're a girl wanting to meet a guy, try classes that are popular with men such as circuits, spinning or any type of combat class. You will also find more guys in the free weights room. If you're a guy wanting to meet a girl, you'll be in the minority and attract a lot of attention if you join a Pilates or yoga class but make sure you're joining for the right reasons!

Work

If you're a girl wanting to meet a guy and you work in a female-dominated environment this isn't going to be such a great option. However, if you work somewhere with a healthy mix of both sexes, then don't let this opportunity slip you by. Take advantage of after-work drinks, parties and social events. You may not want to meet your future husband or wife at work but there may be a colleague who could introduce you to a future spouse. One of my clients was starting a new job and included an important tactic in her dating portfolio strategy. She set herself a target to introduce herself to someone new every day for the first month that she started in her new job. As the new girl, she had the perfect excuse to go up to anyone and everyone.

Evening classes

These are another great way to meet like-minded people but take up an evening class because you have a genuine interest in it, rather than because you want to meet your perfect match in that class.

I had one client who signed up for a basic car mechanics course thinking this would be a great place to meet men – she was sorely disappointed when 80% of her classmates turned out to be women thinking the same thing.

Climbing centers and holidays

If you have a head for heights and a sense of adventure, climbing is a fun activity which attracts a mixed group of men and women who have a down-to-earth approach to life. There is a lot of trust built up since you help and are helped by others in the climbing process. Check out:
www.ukclimbing.com

If you are based outside the UK, you can do an online search using the term "climbing clubs + your city, area or country" in your preferred search engine.

Martial arts

There are many martial arts to choose from and if you're a woman looking for a man, you will have plenty to pick from at martial arts classes. Check out: http://www.martialartsclubs.co.uk/

If you are based outside the UK, you can do an online search using the term "martial arts clubs + your city, area or country" in your preferred search engine.

Environmental volunteering groups

Generally more women take on volunteering in their spare time than men. However, in environmental voluntary groups there is a good mix of both men and women. Some suggestions of environmental voluntary groups in the UK include:

http://www2.btcv.org.uk/display/volunteer The British Trust for Conservation Volunteers

http://www.foe.co.uk/press_for_change/volunteer Friends of the Earth

If you are based outside the UK, you can do an online search using the term "environmental volunteering + your city, area or country" in your preferred search engine.

Church

If you have an affinity with a particular church, they can be great places to build your social network and even meet your spouse. A friend of mine met her now husband through her church and they remain happily married.

Dog-walking

If you've got a dog, you'll know how keen dog owners are to strike up conversations with fellow doggie lovers. Also, if you do have a dog, it can be easier and more fulfilling to meet a perfect match with their very own pooch.

Through friends

To meet potential matches through friends you need to take a proactive approach. Friends will not necessarily introduce you to their single brother or to their husband's single mate. They are more likely to set up introductions and even set you up on blind dates, if you make it clear that you are ready to meet someone and would welcome any introductions that they can suggest.

Where not to meet the opposite sex

The launderette

I have read quite a few relationship books which still advise that you could meet the love of your life over dirty clothes. Come on – how many eligibles have you noticed at your local launderette?

Late-night supermarket shopping:

Another myth is that you will meet your perfect match while cruising the supermarket aisles late at night. Out of the hundreds of single people I have met and worked with, I have never met anyone who has found love while shopping for their groceries.

Through self-development and spiritual groups

The truth is that women spend a lot more time and energy on self and spiritual development. As a woman, you are unlikely to meet the man of your dreams at one of these groups since the ratio is usually 80% women to 20% men. If, however, you are a man with a genuine interest in self or spiritual development, you will have a great selection of women to choose from at any such event.

Trendy bars and clubs

I used to be addicted to the thrill of meeting a total stranger in bars and clubs. It took me years to realize that most of these tall, dark strangers were mainly interested in one thing and that wasn't a long-term relationship.

Restaurants

Whether during the day for lunch or by night for dinner, restaurants are filled with couples, families and groups of girls. Even if you're a guy looking to meet a girl in a restaurant, it is hard to approach anyone when they are sitting with friends on their own designated table.

How to get the most out of online dating

When I first tried online dating in April 2004, I thought I was desperate to be trying it and felt embarrassed telling any of my friends. In November 2004, I met my now husband on a dating site and we got married in August 2005. Since then, more and more of my friends and clients have met their partners online. This is why I urge you to include online dating within your dating portfolio. Check out these statistics:

- Fifteen million people are single in Britain and almost five million are searching for love online (*Guardian, Internet Dating Unplugged, June 29th, 2009*).
- A 2008 online survey conducted by the Matchmaking Services Industry Committee, showed that 45.5% of those surveyed in China have used matchmaking sites, and 32.6% prefer to find a mate on the internet.
- It is estimated that the number of Chinese online daters will reach 140 million by 2010.
- In the US, visits to dating sites rose more than 26% in 2008.

- In the UK, tracking agency Nielsen Online saw the number of visitors to online dating sites rise by 20% in 2008, despite the credit crunch.

I have helped hundreds of men and women find love online and within this section I am including answers to the questions I am most frequently asked about internet dating.

Online dating myths

Myth #1: dating sites are full of losers, liars and players

I'm not going to pretend that dating sites are only frequented by virtuous, integral achievers.

However, as with other places that you could meet your perfect match, you will meet a variety of people and don't tell me that you've never met someone you were extremely attracted to offline who turned out to be a liar, loser or player. The great advantage of online dating is that you have more time to check out someone's credentials through email and speaking to them on the phone before you meet them face to face.

Myth #2: only young people use dating sites

About 30% of my clients are aged above 45 and guess what? They are using online dating sites. There are also a plethora of sites aimed at seniors.

Myth #3: online dating is unsafe

Online dating is actually safer since you initially communicate to users through the dating website rather than giving out your personal email address or phone number. When meeting someone for the first time, you should take the normal precautions: meet in a public place, let friends or family know where you will be and never go home with someone after a first date.

Myth #4: online dating will answer all my problems

I'll stress again that you should not rely upon any one method of meeting potentials and online dating should be included in your dating portfolio along with other methods. You also need to work at online dating in the same way that you need to put time and attention into speed dating, going on blind dates or widening your social circle.

Overcoming your barriers to online dating

Barrier #1: I don't have time to sit at home reading online profiles and checking and replying to emails

I have heard this excuse from so many of my female clients and reply with, "If you were looking for a new job, would you say, 'I haven't got time to send off my CV, update job sites and reply to interview and job offers'?" The main reason that my clients use time as an excuse not to do online dating is because they are actually not ready to go out on the dating scene and need to work through one of their limiting beliefs (see Chapter 3). If you can't find time to devote to online dating then you need to make time. Once you start communicating with a special someone, you will be hooked and won't resent your time spent online.

Barrier #2: I communicate better face to face

The truth is that most people do, but remember that you will get a chance to meet potentials face to face once you have vetted them by email and phone.

Barrier #3: It feels desperate to go online to meet my perfect match

Remember that this was my number one barrier and if I hadn't overcome it, I wouldn't have met my perfect match who, incidentally, had no hang-ups about online dating.

The advantages of online dating

Strength in numbers

Depending on which site you use, you have access to thousands of potentials at the click of a mouse and can email as many as you want.

All in the same boat

Everyone is single so there is no guessing if someone is attached or not as there is when you meet people in bars, at parties or through a mutual interest. If you come across liars who are not single, quickly cease any communication. You can also report them to the site moderation team.

Connect on a different level

It is refreshing to get to know and like someone without the distractions of physical appearance and attraction.

Save time and disappointment

You get to find out about that person through emails and phone calls before you decide if it is worth meeting.

Test their intellect

You can see how well they can write and communicate.

Learn how to communicate with each other

With emails you spend more time thinking about what to write and can be more open because you are not sitting face to face with that person.

Good way to meet men

Men are less likely to try speed dating or singles nights but have less to lose by sitting at home and meeting people online.

Feeling in demand

You can sit back and watch your inbox filling with emails from interested potentials, especially when you first upload your profile.

The dos and don'ts of online dating

Do log on **regularly** since active members show up first in other members' search lists.

Don't write and upload an online profile when you have **just come out of a relationship** and are brimming with **resentment**.

Do exercise **courtesy** and reply to all emails you get. Even if you're not interested, you can use a standard reply such as "Thank you for your email. You're not quite what I am looking for. I wish you every success in your search."

Do be **specific** when emailing users you're interested in and tell them what you like about their profile and exactly what you have in common rather than a generic enquiry such as "Looks like we have lots in common, email me back."

Do **report any rude or nuisance users** to the site moderation team. These teams remove profiles receiving two or three complaints.

Don't reply to people **who ask for your number** without exchanging a few emails first – do you want to date someone who won't make the effort or is only interested in one thing?

Don't agree to **meet anyone in person** until you have exchanged around 10 emails or have been communicating over about 10 days and have got an idea of their beliefs, attitudes and values.

Don't get in touch with people who just **add you to their favorites or send a wink**. Let them be man or woman enough to email you and tell you why they're interested.

Don't expect people you like the look and sound of to get in touch with you if you **add them to your favorites or send a wink**.

Don't **judge people** for their grammar or spelling – would you know how they wrote if you met them face to face?

Do **approach men** online if you are a woman. I would usually advise women looking for a man with predominant masculine energy against making a first move offline. However, the rules are different online and if you don't approach men who you find interesting, you risk missing out on a great opportunity since they may miss your profile amongst the thousands of others posted. I emailed my husband first and he hadn't seen my profile so he was really happy to hear from me.

Do let **men take the lead** after you have sent them an initial email to say you are interested. This includes letting the man ask for your personal email address to write longer emails and asking for your phone number so that you can take the communication to the next level and, of course, asking you out on a first date.

Do **speak to** potential dates over the phone before going on a first date.

Do arrange a shorter date such as **lunch or coffee** if you are at all unsure about your date.

Do let a **friend of family member know** when and where you are meeting someone on a first date.

Do meet in a **public and well-lit place** close to public transport links or easy parking.

Don't **share a lift** home together on a first date.

Writing your online profile

A good online profile is as important to you in meeting your perfect match as is a good CV in landing your dream job. Unfortunately, most online daters don't put the same time and effort into their online profile as they do into their CVs. Here are some tips to help you create your best possible online profile.

- Don't show that you can't be bothered to make the effort with a very short profile or with bits missing, such as this answer which I found on a UK dating site:
  "Why should you get to know Clarissimo?
  Urrr, it's late and a school night so I'll come back to this when there's more time."
- Do make your profile **stand out** with something individual to you and don't stick with the **same old:** like to watch DVDs, go for walks and listen to music. You might think that you will attract a bigger number of potentials by writing a more generic profile but you're looking for "the one" and not "the many".
- Do get a **good friend** to help you with your profile – they'll be much better at selling your qualities. I also offer a profile-writing service to my clients where I am able to draw out your best points and create a profile around these. Contact me for more information on this service.
- Just as you would with a CV, check your profile for spelling mistakes, typos and grammatical errors. Ask a friend or family member to read over your profile and suggest any areas for improvement. If you find you are not getting the responses you want from your profile, make

changes to it and upload a revised version.

- Ladies: be careful not to come across as too desperate in your profile so refrain from mentioning how long you've been single, that online dating is your last resort or that you are you keen to get married or have children.
- Ladies: don't include anything in your profile which suggests that you are not ready for a relationship or don't need a man, such as "I like my independence to do what I want" or "I enjoy travelling on my own and being self-sufficient".
- Guys: if you want to attract a woman with a predominantly feminine energy, don't come across as a best friend type with words such as caring, supportive and sensitive. You may well possess these characteristics, but for your profile you want to emphasize your masculine qualities such as, strength, protection and solidity.
- Don't be **self-deprecating** and, especially if you are a woman, a lack of confidence is a serious turn-off. Men can get away with some self-deprecation since they are perceived as more confident but go lightly and don't overdo putting yourself down or highlighting your faults.
- If you're not naturally witty, don't try to include lots of **humor** in your profile. If jokes and wit come easily to you, you are lucky since most people will warm to a humorous profile.

Exercise 11

Here is a simple process to create your online profile:

1. Think of all the **interests**, **hobbies** and everything that you do outside of work that is **important** to you, for example, reading, theatre, dancing, climbing, yoga, music, travel, gardening, cars, golf, meditation, walking etc.

   Draw out something **specific** about your key interests, which can supply **"hooks"** to people looking at your profile and give them a reason to get in touch with you, for example:

   > "I enjoy **reading** and especially biographies – I've just **read Lewis Hamilton's.**"

   > "My ambition is to **dance** my way around the world, **salsa** in Cuba and **tango** in Argentina."

   > "**Music** is my greatest passion and I am especially into **Motown and jazz.**"

   > "My ideal day would be to go on a long country **walk** stopping for lunch in a cozy pub."

   Create four to five sentences that describe the interests which are most important to you and that you would most like someone to share or appreciate. Include specifics about these interests, which will inspire readers to contact you and ask further questions. Here is an example:

   I've just got back from 2.5 weeks travelling in Thailand and Cambodia, which was far too short to see and do everything. I'm keen to see much more of the world, Tibet, South America, South Africa, to name but a few. I've always wanted to see the Northern Lights and have to go back to Thailand to climb Krabi.

> *I'm relatively new to climbing but it's become a big part of my life. I enjoy a healthy lifestyle and am in good shape but still enjoy a drink or two and a nice big portion of chocolate cake.*
>
> *In my quieter moments, I'm an avid reader including travel literature and autobiographies.*
>
> *An ideal Sunday afternoon for me would be a nice lunch followed by a couple of hours wondering around an interesting exhibition.*

A good way to avoiding continually starting your sentences with "I" is to start them with:

"An ideal day for me…"
"My favorite…"
"My dream…" or
"Friends describe me as…"

2. **List all your qualities** (characteristics and physical attributes), which make you attractive. Get feedback from three or four friends if you are finding this difficult or ask yourself, how would my friends describe me? For example: fun, dry sense of humor, dependable, caring, outgoing, thoughtful, good listener, non crowd pleaser, creative, kind, fit and healthy, tender, sensitive, brave, honest, thoughtful, loyal, generous, strong, having drive and ambition (particularly attractive to women), considerate, affectionate, resourceful, graceful, elegant, adventurous, humble, reliable, responsible, warm, practical, witty, laid-back, easy-going, lively, flexible and understanding.

Even though you will usually tick boxes on the online dating site to describe your **physical appearance** such as height, hair color and eye color, it is a good idea to describe your best physical features to draw potentials in. Describing your best physical features also shows that you have confidence in how you look – a serious turn-on for men and women. For example: youthful looking, tall, petite, slim, curvaceous, broad shouldered, hour-glass figure, blonde, brunette, fair-skinned, olive skin, dark skin, big brown eyes, pretty almond eyes, long eyelashes or long legs.

Create two to three sentences which sum up your qualities. Here is an example: "Friends describe me as fun, loyal, warm and with a good sense of adventure. I'm a curvaceous brunette with striking green eyes."

3. **Write down the most important qualities you are looking for in a date/potential partner.** Steer away from general statements such as kind, reliable and funny, and get specific. For example: I'm looking for someone who has a love for life, likes spending time with friends and family and is always up for new experiences.

Here is an example: "I'm looking for someone with principles (who believes in fidelity and treats people how they would like to be treated) is open-minded, an intrepid traveler and invests in their physical, mental and emotional health."

4. **Put all three sections together.** Your most important interests, your qualities and what you are looking for in a date/potential partner. Take some time to edit until you are happy with your final version.

Here are a couple of good sample profiles to give you some inspiration.

Sample profile #1

My friends and colleagues would describe me as bubbly, fun, spontaneous and with a good sense of humor. I always look on the bright side of life!

I love to seize upon everything that life throws at me – like heading off to Costa Rica with a few days' notice to take part in a charity bike ride and doing a tandem sky-dive over Lake Taupo, New Zealand.

Through work and holidays, I've also travelled to South Korea, Bangladesh, Pakistan, Mozambique, Yemen and South Africa. For me, there's nothing more exhilarating than the challenge of travelling and making yourself understood, even if you don't speak the same language!

Friends and family are also really important to me and they have been instrumental in making me the person I am today. I'm particularly close to my family in Scotland and love spending time with them.

I love my job – and get a bit too passionate sometimes. Working for an international NGO gives me the chance to travel extensively to developing countries and raise funds for fantastic projects.

I'm looking for someone to have lots of adventures with, from discovering new restaurants and museums in Paris to kayaking with dolphins in Australia and everything in between. Home is also very important to me – cooking meals with someone and going for walks in the country. I love the fact that having that special person in your life gives you all sorts of exciting experiences to share together.

I like this profile since it communicates this girl's character and she balances mentioning her love of travel and home. She also makes it clear that she is open and ready for a relationship in her last sentence, "I love the fact that having that special person in your life gives you all sorts of exciting experiences to share together."

Sample Profile #2

I am passionate about rugby, food, music (I play saxophone), good wine and the quality things in life. I am very loyal and caring and also have a wicked sense of humor with a quick wit.

I am tactile and have an underlying romantic streak too. I also believe chivalry is alive and well! I feel I know where I am in life and the baggage has been sent to the refuse site.

I think I have a good balance between my work and my social life and try not to mix the two. I also chair a regional charity raising funds for disadvantaged kids, so my partner needs to be comfortable with sleeves rolled up selling teddy bears at a rugby festival or dressed up for a black tie ball at a royal palace!

Friends say I am at home in any situation, can talk on most subjects but I am a great listener. Friends are very important and I have a very small close knit band, but I will do anything for them.

I believe I am quite successful and secure. I have my own place and am proud of the fact that I maintain it (I actually like ironing and am fussy about starched collars and double cuffs on shirts!!! lol). I'm a pretty good cook too, but tend to use every utensil! (I wash up afterwards though).

I am looking for a lady who has style and a touch of elegance, is happy dressed up or dressed down. A lady who has a degree of independence... in thought and deed. Someone who believes respect is earned, not a right, and wants to care and be cared for.

The person I'm looking for needs to have their own opinions, so I need someone who is not afraid to disagree with me when they need to (actually having read that, that probably means 80% of women!).

My friends and colleagues tell me I can be brutally honest (too much sometimes?), so I think a job in the diplomatic corps is not one I am cut out for. But below the surface I am very tender.

This man does a good job at selling himself to the opposite sex with "I am tactile and have an underlying romantic streak too. I also believe chivalry is alive and well! I feel I know where I am in life and the baggage has been sent to the refuse site." He also mentions that he can iron and cook, which will greatly appeal to women.

Your online photo

It is essential to include a photo with your online profile. If you don't, people will wonder what you've got to hide and, girls, remember that guys are highly visual so need something to look at before they'll make any advances. Profiles with photos get 15 times more replies than those without one. Here are some tips on how to create and select a great online photo.

- Post a recent photo and not one of when you were **much younger** or **looked completely different** – they'll find out the truth when they meet you in the flesh. This is also a form of lying and none of us like meeting liars online!
- Do **change** your photo if you're not attracting enough potentials or if you attract lots of people whom you don't fancy. One of my clients changed his picture to a professional studio shot and started attracting completely different people whom he found attractive!
- For your main photo, pick **a head and shoulders shot** so that online daters can get a good look at your face.
- Wear something **tasteful and sophisticated** in your photo. A photo full of cleavage may attract lots of responses but probably not those interested in a long-term relationship. Guys – wear something which is **smart** but not overly formal unless that is your usual attire.
- Remember to **smile** in your photo, most people look more attractive when they smile and it makes you look more open, friendly and approachable.

- Display at least **two additional photos** of yourself to show different aspects of your life such as showing you doing one of your main interests such as a sport, and one which shows your fun side such as a night shot of you at a party or you on holiday in one of your favorite locations. You can also include a full body shot so that online daters get an idea of the whole package, not just your face.
- Don't post any photos of you posing with **the opposite sex or animals**. A potential could be put off by someone who can't bear to be separated from their dog or who is constantly spending time with the opposite sex.
- Users will be frustrated that they can't get a proper look at you if you are hidden **behind sunglasses or hats.**
- Use **natural daylight** and take the photograph outdoors if possible – flash photography can be less forgiving.
- Don't have **distracting things** in the background of your main photo or anything that might give off the wrong impression – for example, a book shelf behind you when you are not an avid reader.
- If you don't have photo editing software, you can use the free service www.picnik.com which allows you to crop, resize and brighten pictures.

Creating the right username

Your online dating username is very important since it creates a first impression and other users will make assumptions based on your choice. Here are some tips on creating a username which makes the right first impression.

- Use some **originality** and don't add random numbers to your name such as, john12344.
- Don't suggest anything **sexual** such as "sexybeast" unless you are online just to have a good time.
- Think about what is most important for you to communicate to a potential match. This could include your job or profession, an interest, a physical feature such as your hair or body, a word which encapsulates what you stand for or incorporating your name into another word.
- Here are some real life examples of usernames which worked well for the online daters behind them:
    - **Fluteplayer** – for someone who had a passion for music and playing their flute.
    - **Hugster** – for a man who wanted to communicate his warmth and affection.
    - **Legalgem** – for someone whose work in the legal field was very important to them.
    - **Clairendipity** – for someone who believes in serendipity and cleverly combined their name with this word.
    - **Urbanecowarrior** – for someone who is concerned about the environment and likes urban living.
    - **Smartblonde** – for someone who wants to highlight their hair color but also challenge the dumb blonde assumption.

Choosing the right dating site

There are thousands of dating web sites worldwide, which range from those with large databases to those with a more specialist slant such as for those seeking millionaires or a like-minded vegetarian partner.

There are three different strategies which you can take in selecting the right dating site for you.

1. Pick a site with a large database so that you have a wider choice of members to select from. The advantage of picking a website with a larger number of subscribers is that you will have a wider choice of people to choose from within your local area. This is useful if you are restricting your search to a smaller geographical area.
2. Pick a more specialist site with a smaller number of subscribers but who are likely to have more in common with you. The disadvantage of a specialist site is that you may need to cast your net wider in terms or location since there will be fewer subscribers living close to you.
3. Subscribe to both a larger site and a more specialist site.

On the next page are answers to the most common questions I am asked about selecting the right dating site.

Will I improve my chances of meeting someone if I subscribe to more than one dating site?

Yes and no. Yes, you could improve your chances by having access to different subscribers. However, it can be a lot of work to keep up with more than one site and become a full-time job replying to emails and browsing through profiles. It can also be quite costly to pay subscriptions to more than one site. One of my UK clients who had tried using several dating sites at once said that she came across the same guys on all three sites that she subscribed to simultaneously. My recommendation is to sign up to one site at a time and if you're not succeeding with that site to try another one.

How do I choose the right dating site for me?

You haven't got much to lose if you sign up to one of the bigger sites since there is such a wide range of people to choose from. However, if you feel that the bigger sites are not for you then do a search for more specialist sites and take advantage of browsing through the site for free before paying for a subscription. If you see people on a site who you like the look of, then this is a good sign that there may be suitable people on that site for you. Newspaper-owned sites such as Guardian Soulmates or the Times Encounters site, both in the UK, can be good place to meet like-minded people since you have enjoying the same newspaper as a common interest.

Are free dating websites worth a try?

I know people who have had success with free dating sites but remember that you get what you pay for and that people who are looking for a serious relationship are willing to devote time and money to their search.

Suggested UK dating sites

Listed below are a selection of sites which my friends and clients have had success with.

www.datingdirect.com – with more than 5 million members it is the UK's largest and where I met my husband!

www.match.com – the second-largest UK site, has sites worldwide.

www.eharmony.co.uk – get matched with singles based on deep compatibility.

www.natural-friends.com – a specialist website for ethically minded, environmentally sensitive, country-loving, health-conscious, single non-smokers.

www.guardiansoulmates.com – for those who want to be part of a like-minded group of people.

www.encounters.timesonline.co.uk – the dating site of the Times and Times on Sunday newspapers.

www.loveandfriends.com – described by the media as "internet dating for thinking people".

www.countrysidelove.co.uk for country dwellers and lovers.

www.classicalpartners.co.uk for classical music lovers.

www.parentsalready.com for single parents and those interested in meeting someone with a family.

www.yogaromance.com as the name suggests, for those with a love of all things yogic.

www.christianconnection.co.uk – open to singletons of all denominations who put their faith first.

Suggested US dating sites

Listed below is a selection of the most visited US dating sites.

www.singlesnet.com
www.plentyoffish.com
www.eharmony.com
www.true.com
http://personals.yahoo.com/

Suggested European dating sites

Listed below is a selection of the most visited European dating sites.

Spain
http://www.friendscout24.es/

Germany
http://www.edarling.de/

For dating sites in other countries, you can do an online search using the term "dating sites + your country" in your preferred search engine.

Online love stories

Around 75% of my coaching clients meet their perfect match on a dating site. I wanted to share a couple of my favorite success stories to prove to you that it is possible to meet your perfect match online.

> ### Michelle and Pete's story
>
> Michelle and Pete were on the Dating Direct website for about a year before meeting. They had very clear ideas about what they wanted in a partner. Michelle wanted someone who valued trust, honesty and openness and had a warm and caring nature. Pete was looking for care, honesty and sincerity.
>
> Michelle was hooked by this line in Pete's profile: "To be completely honest I just want to fall head over heels in love with someone." Pete loved Michelle's bubbly, go-getter profile and was attracted to her looks.
>
> It was Pete who originally emailed Michelle and asked for her phone number but he could never catch her in. He then sent an email to Michelle with the name of someone else on it. Michelle was really put off and thought Pete was a bit of a player. About a year later, Michelle went back online after a brief relationship and got a message from Pete saying, "Still single?" Michelle didn't realize who it was until they swapped personal emails and she recognized the email address. At this point, she had really fallen for Pete as he had been so funny and engaging. He asked, "Are you going to make me jump through hoops again or do I get your phone number?" Michelle gave it to him and he rang that night.

A week after their initial phone conversation and at the end of an hour and a half telephone conversation, Michelle and Pete set up their first date. Pete took Michelle on a romantic date at a restaurant on the banks of the River Trent. They both felt the chemistry and Pete managed to steal his first kiss.

After their first date, Michelle and Pete continued to text and phone on a daily basis and saw each other two to three times a week. After a month and a half they decided to go on holiday together. This was a real turning point and each night they got closer through long heartfelt chats on the balcony of their apartment. They realized that there was no problem spending time in each other's company and managed to resolve any issues quickly with open communication. A week after they came back from holiday and two months after their initial email, Pete proposed and made Michelle the happiest girl in the world!

They knew from the beginning that they were both what they were looking for in a lifelong partner. They were very honest and upfront about what they wanted and felt. Michelle knew that Pete was the one when he wrote a poem for her beginning, "How can it be after only two dates, I feel in my heart we could be lifelong soul mates."

When Michelle emailed me her story I couldn't stop smiling and as I wrote this I felt such warmth in my heart. It really proves that a soul mate is out there and to keep looking and not give up! It also shows that when you get clear about what you want, that person will come to you.

Jane and Paul's story

Jane really wanted to meet someone to share the rest of her life with and felt like her life was on hold since a lot of her plans involved being in a happy partnership. She also believed that she was a failure for not having met anyone when everyone around her was either getting married or having children. Jane was encouraged by colleagues to give the site Loveandfriends a go and started communicating with Paul whose creative, well-worded and humorous profile she really liked.

When Jane went back online and met Paul she was feeling pretty positive about internet dating since she was meeting and hearing about more and more people who had met their life partners that way. She took a much more relaxed and excited approach than a year earlier when she had become tired and fed up with internet dating. Jane wrote and rewrote her profile and uploaded three flattering and happy-looking photos. Jane says, "Having seen a lot of internet profiles, I can't underestimate how important it is to come across as positive and content and to show that you are serious about meeting someone by writing a thoughtful and well-written profile with no spelling mistakes or typos."

Paul is different from Jane's previous partners since they like doing similar things, are close to each other's families and have a similar attitude towards money and material possessions and they both have a cat!

Jane realized that Paul was the one for her when she took him to meet her family and they all got on really well. For Paul he realized that Jane was his perfect match when they were walking in the mountains together and he realized that he was in love.

Jane was keen not to paint an unrealistic picture and says, "I don't want my story to read like an unobtainable fairy tale; we still have our moments like most couples and we have some differences but work through our challenges and are stronger because of them."

How to get the most out of speed dating

Here is a guide to getting the most out of speed dating.

How speed dating works

Each date lasts around three minutes, based on the psychological theory that this is the amount of time human beings need to decide whether there is chemistry or not. Speed dating organizers usually consider that confidentiality is paramount, so bookings are made online in advance.

Scorecards are provided for daters to enter whether they are interested or not, after each speed date. These are either passed to the speed dating organizer at the end of the speed dating session or participants take them home to be filled in online. Speed daters will be notified by email how many matches they had during the session.

Contact details are only exchanged when both parties agree that they would like to see each other again. If one says no, then it is not listed as a match. Events are usually split into different age groups for example, 23-35, 30-40 and 45-55, and are only run when there are equal numbers of men and women. It is usually set up so that the men at the event move from one woman to another. There is normally time after a speed dating event for everyone to mingle and get to know each other better. There are also specialist speed dating events such as Hindu, Asian Muslim and Christian speed dating and single parent events.

The dos and don'ts of speed dating

Do show courtesy to everyone at the event

Even if you find someone unattractive or obnoxious, people you could be interested in will be watching your behavior throughout the evening.

Don't get drunk

You'll know from your teenage days that alcohol seriously impairs your judgment. It is also a serious turn-off to be propositioned by someone who is slurring their words or unsteady on their feet.

Do focus on the other person

Show interest in everyone you speak to; we all like to feel like we are the centre of attention.

Don't hang around with your friends all night

Even the most confident of guys will be put off by a large group of single girls.

Top speed dating questions

Be wary of asking **overly clever or long-winded questions**. At a speed dating event, I was once asked, "With which historical character do you most identify?" It wasn't the kind of question I had time to answer in three minutes and nor did I have much inclination to answer it when I was out for some fun and excitement.

Avoid using **closed questions**, which can be answered with "yes" or "no" and bring the conversation to a halt. Closed questions usually begin with "do" and "is/are".

Avoid any **leading questions**, which make an assumption about the other person, such as, "You seem like a fit person, do you do a lot of sport?"

Avoid any overly **personal questions** or ones which make the other person feel **vulnerable**, such as, "How long have you been single?"

It is worth preparing questions and answers in advance of a speed dating event so that you don't become tongue-tied in those vital three minutes.

Here are some suggested questions which are inoffensive and allow you to find out more about the other person:

Finding out more about the other person:

- What do you do for a living? Where do you work?
- What do you like doing outside of work?
- What are you passionate about?
- What/who is most important to you in your life?
- What do you consider your best attributes?
- What are the most important things you are looking for in a person?

Finding out more about the other person's hobbies and interests

- What do you like doing in your free time?
- What kind of music do you like?
- What sports do you enjoy watching and participating in?
- What was the last film you saw?
- What is your favorite film?
- What did you do last weekend?
- What would your ideal Sunday be?
- What has been your best holiday?
- Where would you most like to go on holiday?

Fun questions

- If you won the lottery, how would you spend it?
- What or who makes you laugh?
- If you could live anywhere in the world, where would it be?
- What is the most adventurous thing you have ever done?
- What is one of the biggest risks you have taken in your life?

Speed dating sites in the UK

http://www.speeddater.co.uk/
http://www.smartdatinguk.com/
http://www.xfactordates.com/speeddating/uk/

Speed dating sites in the US

http://www.fastlife.com/
http://www.speeddate.com/

Speed dating in other countries

For speed dating sites in other countries, you can do an online search using the term "speed dating + your country or your city" in your preferred search engine.

How to get the most out of introduction agencies

How does it work?

Processes can vary from agency to agency so go to individual agencies' websites to check for yourself. Here is a typical introduction agency process:

- The agency sets up a face-to-face meeting or telephone call with you to find out about you and the type of person you would like to meet.

- The agency will write a profile for you based on answers to your questions in your initial meeting. This profile usually includes some of your weaknesses as well as your strengths to paint a realistic picture.
- The agency will then select suitable partners for you based on your criteria.
- Once the agency has found a match that you are interested in and see as compatible, they will send you a profile and contact number for that person.
- After each meeting the agency will get feedback and do another search if your date is not compatible or you don't feel any chemistry.

Membership levels, options and terms and conditions

You need to refer to individual dating agencies to understand their membership levels, options and terms and conditions. However, there are usually a number of options which you can choose from:
- The agency can select introductions for you and, depending on which membership level you select and how much you pay, you can have from four to eight selections over 12-24 months.
- Some agencies offer a cheaper passive membership where you are not matched with potentials but your profile is available for members to view. There are usually restrictions on this type of membership.
- Some agencies offer a more costly bespoke matchmaking service.
- Fees to UK introduction agencies vary so you need to contact them directly to understand their pricing structure.

Dos and don'ts of using an introduction agency

- **Do** select an agency that offers a **free introductory meeting.**
- **Do** select an agency that is a member of **a professional body**, such as the Association of British Introduction Agencies in the UK, www.abia.org.uk
- **Don't** join an agency that is **guarded** about its pricing and membership levels.
- **Do** select an agency based on a **recommendation**.

> **Susan's story**
>
> "I would definitely recommend introduction agencies. I joined the UK-based **Attractive Partners**, which is not the most costly on the market although some may think it's expensive. They have done what they said they would do and have provided me with four dates up to now. I think as with most things you get what you pay for.
>
> They are very professional, easy to talk to and because they are all women they understand where I am coming from. The biggest plus point for me is that they have only matched me with men who meet my criteria – I do not have to filter through unsuitables and spend time wondering if they want the same things as me. The men the agency have introduced me to have been of a very high standard – high achievers, solvent, intelligent and articulate. It may be that men who join an agency are generally of a higher standard or it may be that the agency filters out the less appealing ones.
>
> I like the complete confidentiality I get from an agency so I don't have to put a profile online and declare my innermost desires to the whole world."

Suggested UK introduction agencies

Listed below is a selection of sites which clients have recommended

> http://www.attractivepartners.co.uk – with bases in London and across the UK.
>
> http://www.drawingdownthemoon.co.uk/ – well-established, London-based introduction agency.
>
> http://www.seventy-thirty.com/ – a matchmaking and partner headhunting company for successful and affluent people.

Introduction agencies in other countries

For introduction agencies in other countries, you can do an online search using the term "introduction agency + your country or your city" in your preferred search engine.

Good luck creating your dating portfolio strategy and getting out there and meeting potentials!

Chapter 8

Maximizing your chances of meeting your perfect match

Neither I nor my clients have had an easy time on the way to meeting our perfect matches. I've let past partners treat me in a way that now makes me cringe and I've treated partners in a way that now makes me feel ashamed. Some of my clients have persisted with online dating for two to three years before meeting their perfect match. Other clients have remained determined not to let their painful pasts dictate their futures. What myself and these clients have in common is that we have now met our perfect matches, are happier than ever and realize that the time and effort we put into finding our ideal relationship was all worthwhile. You may still be feeling slightly skeptical about your chances of meeting your perfect match after reading Chapters 1-7. If so, read on for inspiration and encouragement to keep going.

Eight ways to stay motivated while searching for your perfect match

If you've received your fair amount of rejection, every man/woman you meet isn't right for the long term and you've tried every single dating option out there, you could ask, "What's the point?" But DON'T. Despite Jenson

Button's promising early career starting in 1988 and after enduring much criticism and disappointment, he didn't win the Grand Prix World Championship until 2009. Button persevered, maintained belief and stayed focused on his way to winning the World Championship. You too need to stay focused and motivated in order to meet that special someone.

#1: Stay focused and let go of attachment

When you really want something in life, there is a danger of trying too hard to get it and coming across as desperate. The problem with focusing too much on what you want is that you inevitably end up focusing more on what you don't want. Examples include "I want to lose weight" becoming "I don't want to look fat"; "I want to earn money" becoming "I don't want to have to worry about money anymore", "I want to meet my perfect match" becoming "I don't want to be sad and lonely for the rest of my life". The law of attraction works in a way where like attracts like so if we focus on what we want, we are more likely to get it. We tend to focus more energy on what we don't want so inevitably that is what we attract.

I know from experience that when you really want to attract your perfect match into your life that it can be incredibly difficult to stop focusing on the negatives of feeling lonely, your biological clock ticking or having no one to go on holiday with. You do, however, need to let go of some attachment to your goal by staying focused but being open to possibilities and trusting that your persistence and belief will pay off.

> "You can look at every problem you have in your life as an opportunity for some greater benefit. You can stay alert to opportunities by being grounded in the wisdom of uncertainty. When your preparedness meets opportunity, the solution will spontaneously appear."
>
> — Deepak Chopra, *The Seven Spiritual Laws of Success*

Letting go of attachment and focusing on what you want rather than don't want is one of the biggest challenges we face in our lives and can be hard to face on our own. I highly recommend the book, *Ask and It Is Given, Learning to Manifest Your Desires,* by Esther and Jerry Hicks, The Teachings of Abraham, to help you better understand and use the Law of Attraction to meet your perfect match.

#2: Act as if you are with your perfect match

Acting as if you are already with your perfect match sends a subliminal message to others that you are ready to start a relationship. There is something very attractive about someone who has space and is ready to welcome a special someone into their life. Here are some suggestions as to how you can "act as if."

- Wear some sexy lingerie rather than gray and misshapen underwear.
- Treat yourself to something that you would normally splash out on for a partner such as a special birthday or Christmas present.

- Cook yourself a tasty meal just as you would for a partner.
- Break your routine and do something different, such as going to the theatre, a comedy night, a new restaurant, sports event or outdoor activity.

#3: Be the person you want to meet

Opposites do attract, like masculine and feminine energy as mentioned in Chapter 5. However, potential partners will be turned off by men or women who feel incomplete and are looking for someone to make up for their failings, such as lack of money, self-esteem or excitement in their lives. If you are not feeling whole and looking for "your other half", focus on how you can become more of a complete person before meeting your perfect match.

#4: Maintain self-esteem

Self-esteem can ebb and flow as potentials come and go. It is, however, so important to maintain self-esteem as potential partners will run a mile from anyone who is coming across as insecure and unconfident. Go back to Chapter 1 to reread tips about maintaining self-esteem.

#5: Don't settle for second best

When you have been searching for your perfect match for a long time and are really craving the company of the opposite sex, it can be tempting to lap up the attention of an admirer, get to like them and then get more involved while ignoring the fact that they do not match up to your "really want list" or share similar values, beliefs and vision. The biggest danger of settling for second best is that the longer you stay with that person, the harder it becomes to end the relationship and the more time you spend with them, the longer it will take you to meet your perfect match. Staying in a second-best relationship will lower your self-esteem and confidence to meet the right person.

#6: Stay positive

You may be sick of hearing the mantra "think positive", but the fact remains that those who do maintain a positive mental attitude achieve greatness against all odds. They are also the "radiators" in life who people warm to.

#7: Get flirty

Flirting is all about playfulness and doesn't necessarily have to be sexual in its intention. It can be the interest and charm you show towards a total stranger, child or even towards an animal. When we act in a playful way, we become less serious, forget about our woes and come across as more light-hearted. This is exactly the type of energy which first attracts us to someone of the opposite sex so make an intention to go out there and flirt.

#8 Spend time with other single people

You can reach a certain age where all your friends are in relationships or married with children. I am not suggesting that you sether ties with married friends but am recommending that you balance your time spent with them, meeting and hanging out with single people. You are unlikely to meet the man or woman of your dreams whilst spending time with your friends' children in the park. If your single friends are one by one pairing off, then read about suggestions for joining social networks in **Chapter 7**.

The fourteen mistakes to avoid in the early stages of a relationship

You've met someone you're attracted to and with whom you see some long-term potential. The only problem is that you are worried about blowing it in the early stages. Here are 14 mistakes to avoid.

Mistake #1: You see potential in your new date but know that there are some things that they would have to change in order for the relationship to work in the long term, such as become more reliable, make more time for you, end a relationship they are currently in, get a better job, be more positive or let go of strong ties with their mother. Don't make the mistake of thinking that you are capable of changing someone's basic attitudes or behaviors.

Mistake #2: Don't talk about your ex or exes with excessive fondness or resentment. This clearly signals that you haven't moved on and don't yet have space for a new partner.

Mistake #3: Don't talk about plans too far into the future, such as getting married or having children within the first 10 dates.

Mistake #4: Don't relax too much within the first 10 dates by turning up for a date in chill-out clothes such as tracksuit bottoms or without doing your hair and make-up.

Mistake #5: Don't try to make the other person fall in love with you by splashing out on expensive gifts. You cannot MAKE someone fall in love with you.

Mistake #6: If you are a woman, don't agree to have sex within the first 10 dates.

Mistake #7: If you are a man, don't come on too strong physically within the first 10 dates.

Mistake #8: Don't agree to see him or her at your home late at night without going on a date first. This could encourage future booty calls and sex without wining and dining you first is for casual not serious relationships.

Mistake #9: Don't make surprise visits to your new partner at home or work. This could be interpreted as inappropriate and even as a form of stalking.

Mistake #10: Give your new partner some space and don't call, text or email them excessively.

Mistake #11: Don't to be tempted to fall into the habit of seeing each other every night. This can make the relationship develop too quickly without both of you truly enjoying the uncertainty and romance of the courting stage.

Mistake #12: Don't make the mistake of having such a full diary that you don't have time for your new partner.

Mistake #13: Don't make the mistake of always being available to your new partner at a moment's notice. This could encourage your partner to use you when their other plans fall through.

Mistake #14: Don't move in with your partner without some kind of commitment, whether it be engagement, marriage or commitment to have children (if you want them).

How to tell if he/she is into you

Part of the thrill of a new relationship is about not knowing how the other person feels about you. Things may seem to be going well but you're not 100% sure whether he/she is genuinely into you. A "where is the relationship going" talk could make someone run a mile at this stage, so here are some signs to look out for which signal they're into you.

- They show commitment by calling/answering calls every day and sending thoughtful text messages.
- They make time to see you at the weekend.
- They make time for you by not rushing off at the end of a date or suggesting longer dates such as a whole day out at the weekend.

- They give up another plan to spend time with you.
- They tell you that they like or love you.
- They give you thoughtful but not necessarily extravagant gifts.
- They say that they will miss you if either of you go away for a period of time.
- They stay in touch while one of you is away for a period of time.
- They show/respond to physical affection in public such as holding hands, kissing or hugging.
- They introduce you to their friends or family.
- They go out of their way to plan a special or unusual date.
- They are willing to wait before having sex.
- They open up and show signs of intimacy by sharing vulnerabilities or secrets (but also be wary of someone trying to manipulate you in this way).
- They show signs of high energy and don't complain about being tired when you have, for example, stayed up until 5am talking.
- They follow through on promises, such as taking you to a special place which they have previously said, they must take you to.

Fourteen ways to maintain a healthy relationship

After spending considerable time and energy meeting your perfect match you will want to do everything you can to ensure the long-term success of this relationship.

The chance of a first marriage ending in divorce over a forty-year period is 67%. Half of all divorces will occur in the first seven years.

The divorce rate for second marriages can be as much as 10% higher than for first ones.

The main reason that so many marriages inevitably end in divorce is down to one factor, complacency, which manifests itself in taking the other person for granted. Continued complacency in a romantic relationship leads to that dull, stuck-in-a-rut feeling, which leaves you dissatisfied; you will eventually go elsewhere to fulfill your basic needs for love, sex and affection.

How can you avoid the trap of complacency in your relationships and keep the sparks flying?

1. **Practice an attitude of gratitude**

   Being genuinely grateful for all that your partner gives, says and does for you is fundamental. Gratitude needs to be practiced on a regular basis and can be expressed in simple words, such as "Thank you for that delicious meal which we shared together." It can also be expressed in more grandiose ways such as buying gifts or flowers for your partner at times other than birthdays, Valentine's Day, anniversaries or Christmas. It can be expressed physically with hugs, foot rubs and massages.

2. **Remind yourselves often of what brought you together**

   Focusing on why you came together reminds you of your special bond and will help when thoughts turn to "the grass could be greener with someone else or if I was single."

3. **Don't become a slave to routine**

   Rigid routine can drain the blood out of the healthiest of relationships, because it is the opposite of spontaneity, which sparks romance and passion. Avoid always going to the same restaurants or other places because they're easy to get to. If you're staying in, do something different apart from lounging in front of the TV, from time to time. This could include talking over a home-made candlelit dinner, listening to music, dancing to music, playing board games, enjoying a cheese and wine evening or exchanging sensual massages.

   Enjoy the adventure of discovering new places just as you did when you first started dating.

   Avoid a sex life driven by routine, this can include experimenting making love at different times of day rather than always when you go to bed or wake up in the morning. Vary where you make love, whether it is in different rooms around the house or in locations away from home and vary positions and which of you initiates sex.

   These are all things that we do in the first throes of love, but easily get out of the habit of doing once we're settled and comfortable.

4. **Indulge in surprise, spontaneity and fun**

    Surprise, spontaneity and fun keep you on your toes and make your heart skip a beat when you first get involved with someone. You're not sure when they're going to call, you are surprised by the intensity of that first kiss, you're delighted when you're taken to new places, introduced to new people and try out new things. Remember what you were like and what you did when you first got together and try reenacting some of those special times. This could include going back to the place where you went on your first date, spending a whole day or evening in bed together with no distractions, going for romantic walks in nature, taking baths together, phoning each other when you are not together, or if you have children getting a babysitter and going out, just the two of you.

5. **Show your love for each other**

    After a while it can be all too easy to think that there is no need to say or show your love to your partner, since it is a given and you wouldn't still be with them if you didn't love them. Everyone has a basic need to feel loved; we don't stop telling our children how much we love them because we see them every day, nor should we stop telling our partners how much we love them. Women especially like to hear loving words and sentiments from their partners, such as "I love you" or "I am totally committed to you". Men especially like to be appreciated for what they contribute in a relationship such as practical tasks they carry out or for working long hours.

Love can also be expressed in loving deeds which you carry out for your partner such as cooking them their favorite homemade dinner, picking them up after a late night out or fixing their laptop. Love can also be shown through the physical affection you share such as hugging, kissing, stroking and massaging your partner. Finally, thoughtful gifts can express how much you care about your partner.

6. **Act, think and behave sexily**
   Dress to impress, even around the house. Invest in sexy underwear – a good return on investment is guaranteed! Pamper yourself with facials, pedicures, manicures, grooming, exercise, saunas and steams. Fantasize about each other when you are together and alone.

7. **Spend time apart and give each other space**
   It's true that absence makes the heart grow fonder. Spending time apart makes you realize how special each other are and is a real aphrodisiac!

8. **Maintain a balance of "me time", "family time" and "us time"**
   Maintaining your own interests and passions mean that you will have things to talk about and share, which are inspiring and bring life to the relationship. However, it is important to not let "me time" take priority over "us time", which should be time spent alone as a couple without friends or family. If you have children, it is important to also make time to be together as a family rather than one parent often looking after the kids while the other goes off and does "me time."

9. **Those who sleep together stay together**
   Stress, work commitments, hormonal changes and young children can all affect our desire or energy levels to make love. However, if you notice that the quality or frequency of your lovemaking has significantly decreased, you need to address this important part of your relationship. There are usually other underlying relationships issues which point to the reason why your lovemaking has diminished and these need to be confronted.

10. **Spend more time listening than talking**
    Do you remember how you listened intently to your partner during the early stages of your relationship? You waited on their every word and were dying to hear more about what they did, felt and thought. As relationships develop, we lose this enthusiasm to listen and can end up misinterpreting and misunderstanding our partners. Listening to someone without interruption is one of the greatest gifts you can share.

11. **Working at a relationship takes more than one person**
    You may have grown sick of hearing "You need to work at a relationship". What people fail to say is "You both need to work at a relationship". If you feel like you are putting all the effort in or your partner is, then you need to redress the balance. No single person in a relationship can ensure its success. It is a partnership where both parties contribute.

12. **Show affection for each other every day**
    It is the small consistent gestures such as always kissing your partner good-bye in the mornings

which have been proven to keep couples together rather than grandiose ones such as lavish holidays or expensive nights out. Cuddling up together at bed time is another ritual which will maintain connection between you and your partner.

13. **Discuss and work out your conflict strategy**
It doesn't matter how you resolve conflict in your relationship as long as that strategy works for both parties. You may have grown up in a house where shouting was the norm so resolving conflict with raised voices works well for you. It may not work well for your partner who grew up in a household where raised voices led to physical violence between her parents. You need to both be honest about how specific behaviors during conflict make you feel. For example, if taking time out makes you feel calmer and more prepared to deal with issues, then let your partner know this so they can accommodate it. If you find yourself switching off to a raised voice and more forceful body language, discuss with your partner how they could better influence you by lowering their voice and being less forceful with their gestures.

Why you should never give up on your dream of meeting your perfect match

You may have read this book; felt momentarily inspired and then reverted back to your same old thinking.

"I've been single and trying to meet someone for years; maybe meeting someone is just not my lot in life."

"It's alright for the people mentioned in this book, they're not me and they're not in MY situation."

"I don't feel strong enough to put myself through more rejection and disappointment."

"There must be something wrong with me; everyone else I know is settled or married with children."

"If I stop thinking about meeting someone, it will just happen."

"I'm quite happy on my own with a good social life, being able to do what I want and not having to answer to anyone else."

"I don't even want a relationship if it's like the ones I see my friends in."

"With my job, family and active social life, I don't have the time to spend looking for my perfect match."

All of the above are based on fear and are lame excuses not to pursue your dream of meeting your perfect match which will make you happier than a vibrant social life and feel more fulfilling than a successful career. I know that you have the determination, strength and bravery to let go of these excuses and get what you really want.

It usually takes time, work, determination and persistence to meet your perfect match. When you do meet them, you will realize that all that effort was well and truly worthwhile as you experience a type of love, happiness, security and peace which you have never felt before. There will be no more feeling like something is missing in your life and no more anxiety about when you are finally going to meet your life partner.

Those determined to realize their dreams don't give up easily. It took the inventor James Dyson five years and 5,127 attempts before he created his working prototype.

It took a further five years of rejection before he launched what was to become the best-selling vacuum cleaner in the world. Dame Kelly Holmes came from a humble background and showed athletic potential from an early age. She went into the army to serve her country before deciding to prepare for the Olympics. Just as she thought her dreams of competing in the Olympics were coming to fruition, she suffered minor injuries and was diagnosed with cancer. Despite a life-threatening disease and injuries, she went on to win two gold medals at the Athens Olympics in 2004. All the people who are mentioned in the examples and stories throughout this book have thought about giving up more than once but persisted with their dream of spending the rest of their lives with a very special person; they are all grateful for having kept going since now they are living in previously unimagined happiness.

I wish you every success in meeting your perfect match; don't give up along the way.

Candy

Disclaimer

We at www.howtomeetyourperfectmatch.com (also referred to as "the proprietors" or "we" from herein) are committed to providing accurate and as broadly inclusive information as possible to our readers.

Continuing to read further means that you understand and accept responsibility for your own actions, thus releasing the proprietors from all liability. The product herein offers information and suggestions, neither of which must be followed or attempted. Whatever you do is your decision and in no way are we responsible for your actions or any ideas you may have gained, directly or indirectly, from reading this product.

The proprietors believe that the content of this product are accurate, complete and current as of the date of publication and the proprietors make no warranty or representation as to the accuracy, completeness, or currency of the content of this product, either as of the date of publication or at any time thereafter. Readers of the content of this product are solely responsible for the verification of any content prior to their reliance on the content published therein.

Other sites: www.howtomeetyourperfectmatch.com and www.howtomeetyourperfectmatch.co.uk are not responsible for the contents of any off-site pages or any other sites linked to this product, www.howtomeetyourperfectmatch.com and www.howtomeetyourperfectmatch.co.uk expressly disclaims all liability for images, content and opinion expressed on other sites that may be accessed through links within this product.

Likewise, www.howtomeetyourperfectmatch.com and www.howtomeetyourperfectmatch.co.uk disclaims all liability for images, content and opinion expressed on outside sites that choose to link to this product.

ACKNOWLEDGEMENTS

I must firstly mention my beloved husband, Ian Jannetta-Porter, who is a rock, inspiration and constant motivation for me and without whom I would never have been able to write this book. Secondly, my young son, Luca Jannetta-Porter, who has provided me with love and joy throughout the process of writing this book. Thirdly, my friend Sharon Shields who motivated me to write this book, constantly gave advice and wisdom and who continues to inspire me. I would especially like to mention Naazi Marouf and Paul Godden who took time out from their busy lives to read a first draft of this book and who provided invaluable feedback. I owe enormous gratitude to all my coaching clients and all those who have attended my workshops; you have all inspired and touched me in your own special way.

www.ingramcontent.com/pod-product-compliance
Lightning Source LLC
Chambersburg PA
CBHW050636300426
44112CB00012B/1816